First People

First People

WRITTEN BY **DAVID C. KING**
CONSULTANT **PETER M. WHITELEY**

LONDON, NEW YORK, MUNICH,
MELBOURNE, AND DELHI

Editor **JOHN SEARCY**
Senior Designer **TIA ROMANO**
Additional Design **MARK JOHNSON DAVIES,**
BILL MILLER, JESSICA PARK
Managing Art Editor **MICHELLE BAXTER**
Art Director **DIRK KAUFMAN**
Publishing Director **BETH SUTINIS**
Production Manager **IVOR PARKER**
DTP Coordinator **KATHY FARIAS**
Picture Researcher **ANNE BURNS**
Cartographer **ED MERRIT**

First Edition, 2008

08 09 10 11 12 10 9 8 7 6 5 4 3 2 1

Published in the United States by
DK Publishing
375 Hudson Street
New York, New York 10014

Copyright © 2008 Dorling Kindersley Limited

Published in Great Britain by Dorling Kindersley Limited.

DK books are available at special discounts when
purchased in bulk for sales promotions, premiums,
fund-raising, or educational use. For details, contact:

DK Publishing Special Markets
375 Hudson Street
New York, NY 10014
SpecialSales@dk.com

A catalog record for this title is available
from the Library of Congress.

ISBN 978-0-7566-4092-7

Color reproduction by Colourscan, Singapore

Printed and bound
in China by Hung Hing

Discover more at
www.dk.com

CONTENTS

INTRODUCTION

What do you think of when you hear the words *American Indian?* For many people, the phrase conjures up a series of conflicting images. You might think of warriors in headdresses riding across the Plains, or kachina dancers performing in the Pueblo villages of the Southwest. You might think of famous leaders such as Geronimo or Sitting Bull, or famous events such as the First Thanksgiving or the Trail of Tears. You might also think of things from the modern world, such as the Indian casinos that have spread across the country, or the pow-wows that are held throughout the year. However, regardless of what images come to mind when you think of American Indians, you may have trouble putting them together. How do the owners of the casinos relate to the riders in the headdresses? How does the First Thanksgiving, when the Indians got along so well with the Pilgrims, relate to the violent battles that took place on the Plains?

One problem that makes it difficult to understand the world of American Indians is that they have never existed as a single culture. When Europeans arrived in North America in the 16th century, the country was inhabited by hundreds of different tribes, with hundreds of different ways of life. Of course, tribes that lived near each other had many things in common, but a Cherokee from the Southeast mountains and a Haida from the Northwest coast would have been puzzled if you told them they were both part of a group called "Indians." Even today, when Indians from many tribes work and celebrate together, they still maintain their distinct tribal identities. This book looks at the cultures of American Indians region by region, showing how all of them found their own answers to the questions of where to live, what was important to them, and how to survive.

INDIANS OR NATIVE AMERICANS?

When Columbus arrived in the Americas in 1492, he called the people he encountered *Indians,* because he thought he had sailed to Asia. Later, the term *American Indian* was used to refer to America's Native people to differentiate them from people living in India. In the 20th century, some people have argued that the phrase *Native American* is preferable, since the word *Indian* is associated with many negative stereotypes. However, most of the people in question still call themselves *Indians*—or by their specific tribe name. Today, both *American Indian* and *Native American* are considered acceptable.

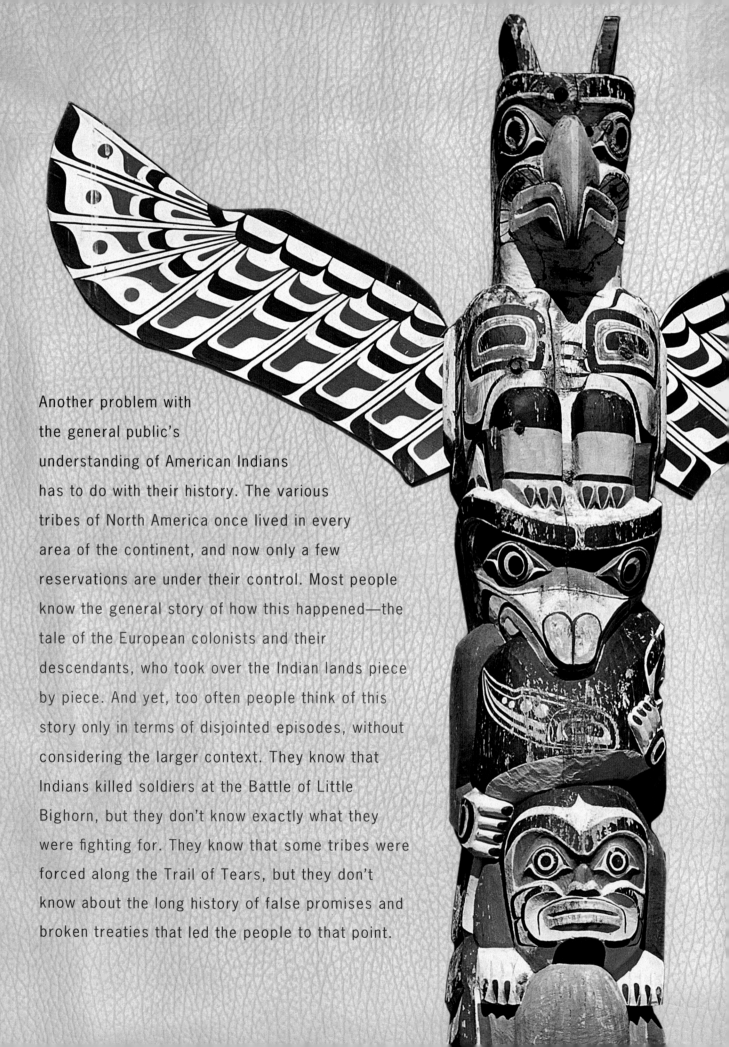

Another problem with the general public's understanding of American Indians has to do with their history. The various tribes of North America once lived in every area of the continent, and now only a few reservations are under their control. Most people know the general story of how this happened—the tale of the European colonists and their descendants, who took over the Indian lands piece by piece. And yet, too often people think of this story only in terms of disjointed episodes, without considering the larger context. They know that Indians killed soldiers at the Battle of Little Bighorn, but they don't know exactly what they were fighting for. They know that some tribes were forced along the Trail of Tears, but they don't know about the long history of false promises and broken treaties that led the people to that point.

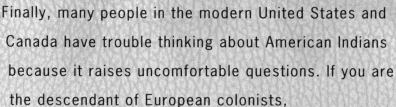

Finally, many people in the modern United States and Canada have trouble thinking about American Indians because it raises uncomfortable questions. If you are the descendant of European colonists, how should you feel about the fact that your ancestors may have contributed to the destruction of hundreds of Native cultures? If you live in modern-day Virginia, how should you feel about the fact that the land you call home was taken from the Powhatans, and dozens of neighboring tribes? These are not easy questions to think about, and this book cannot provide the answers.

Many questions involving American Indians are difficult for other Americans to think about.

However, it can give you a clearer understanding of who America's first people were, what happened to them during the European conquest, and how they have managed to preserve and renew their many traditional cultures in the 21st-century world.

INDIAN CULTURE REGIONS

Before the arrival of Europeans, North America was home to hundreds of individual tribes, which occupied 10 basic culture regions. These regions have been defined by modern experts, based on geography, climate, and shared cultural practices. On this map, each region is paired with a tool or work of art created by one of the many diverse societies who called that region home.

The Plateau was a hilly area, whose rivers swam with salmon. This Ntlakyapamuk deer figure was made from the bark of the rush plant.

The Pacific Northwest was a forested area along the coast. This Nuxalk mask displays the exceptional woodworking skills of the area's many tribes.

The Great Plains were home to huge herds of bison. This ceremonial Blackfoot skull shows the importance the local tribes put on the animal.

California had a mild climate and an abundance of wild foods. This Pomo flail was used to knock acorns and other seeds out of trees and bushes.

The Great Basin was a harsh, arid region whose people had to struggle to survive. This Ute pendant is shaped like a lizard, which represented long life.

The Southwest was a desert environment that was home to many advanced cultures. These Hopi Kachina dolls were given to young girls by ceremonial dancers.

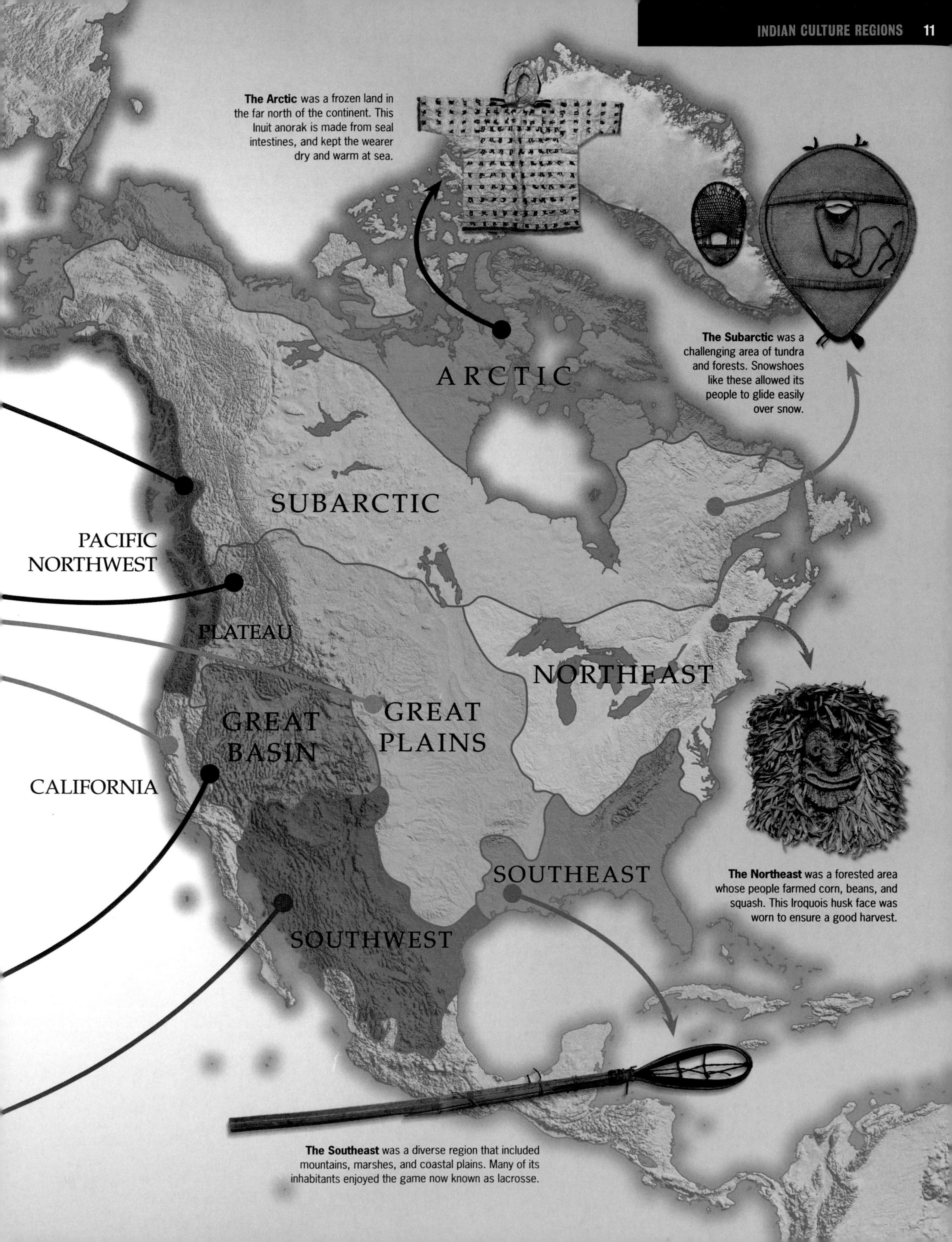

The Arctic was a frozen land in the far north of the continent. This Inuit anorak is made from seal intestines, and kept the wearer dry and warm at sea.

The Subarctic was a challenging area of tundra and forests. Snowshoes like these allowed its people to glide easily over snow.

ARCTIC

SUBARCTIC

PACIFIC
NORTHWEST

PLATEAU

NORTHEAST

GREAT
BASIN

GREAT
PLAINS

CALIFORNIA

SOUTHEAST

The Northeast was a forested area whose people farmed corn, beans, and squash. This Iroquois husk face was worn to ensure a good harvest.

SOUTHWEST

The Southeast was a diverse region that included mountains, marshes, and coastal plains. Many of its inhabitants enjoyed the game now known as lacrosse.

TIMELINE

The story of American Indians spans thousands of years, from the arrival of humans during the Ice Age to the protests of the 1970s. There's no way to capture all the events in just two pages, but this timeline shows some of the high points and low points that have shaped the history of a people.

8000 BCE Ice Age ends; mammoths become extinct.

(BCE) 18,000   10,000

---

300 Maya culture rises Mesoamerica.

750 Mississippian culture begins, lasts until 1600.

1200 Anasazi build Mesa Verde Cliff Palace.

1428 Aztec Empire becomes dominant state in central Mexico.

1492 Columbus lands in West Indies, names the natives "Indians."

(CE) 500   1000   1100   1200   1300   1400   1500   1510   1520   1530

300–700 Hopewell civilization flourishes.

900 Anasazi civilization develops in Southwest.

1000 Pueblo communities of Acoma and Hopi established.

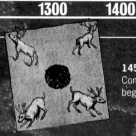

1450 Iroquois Confederacy begins.

1513 Ponce de León lands in Florida.

1521 Second Ponce de León expedition forced to evacuate Florida by Calusa Tribes.

1636–37 Pequot War fought against the English.

1673 Louis Joliet and Jacques Marquette explore Mississippi River.

1680 Pueblo Revolt led by Popé drives Spanish out of New Mexico.

1685 French establish Fort Saint Louis in Texas.

1715–17 Yamasee War fought between South Carolina colonists and Southeast tribes.

1630   1640   1650   1660   1670   1680   1690   1700   1710   1720

1646 Powhatans defeated by English in Virginia.

1675–76 King Philip's War fought; Wampanoags and Narragansetts slaughtered and enslaved.

1682 La Salle claims Louisiana for France.

1700 Navajo acquire sheep, later leading to wool blankets.

1821 Sequoyah invents Cherokee alphabet.

1832 Black Hawk's War fought in Midwest.

1863–64 Navajo rounded up by U.S. Army in Southwest and forced to make "Long Walk" to Bosque Redondo, near Fort Sumner.

1876 Custer and 7th Cavalry defeated by Sioux at Little Bighorn.

1879 Carlisle School founded in Pennsylvania to assimilate Indians into white society.

1887 Dawes Act divides reservations into individual holdings and opens millions of acres to white settlement.

1820   1830   1840   1850   1860   1870   1880   1890   1900   1910

1831–39 Cherokee and other Southeast tribes forced to relocate to Indian Territory along "Trail of Tears."

1868 United States abandons some forts following defeat in Red Cloud's War.

1877 Chief Joseph's band of Nez Perce surrender after avoiding capture for nearly 1,000 miles (1,600 km).

1886 General Nelson A. Miles accepts surrender of Apache warriors led by Geronimo.

1890 Sioux Ghost Dancers massacred by units of 7th Cavalry at Wounded Knee, South Dakota.

5000 BCE Inuit and Aleut people migrate to North America.

3000 BCE Red-Paint People flourish in Northeast.

1000 BCE Adena culture begins.

9000   8000   7000   6000   5000   4000   3000   2000   1000   500

9000 BCE Folsom culture follows after Clovis.

5300 BCE Settled farming communities established in Mesoamerica.

3500 BCE Farming spreads to present-day United States.

1500 BCE Olmec culture develops in Mesoamerica, lasts until 400 BCE.

1540–42 Francisco de Coronado leads Spanish as far north as Kansas.

1598–1606 Juan de Oñate founds Spanish settlements in New Mexico and treats Indians brutally.

1608 Samuel de Champlain establishes colony of New France, with capital at Quebec City.

1540   1550   1560   1570   1580   1590   1600   1610   1620   1630

1536 Jacques Cartier trades fur with Indians on the St. Lawrence River.

1539–42 Hernando de Soto lands in Florida and explores Southeast.

1585–87 English establish colonies on Roanoke Island.

1590 John White discovers all Roanoke colonists have disappeared.

1607 English establish colony at Jamestown, Virginia.

1620 English Pilgrims land at Plymouth.

1750 Great Plains tribes revolutionized by adoption of horses.

1763 Pontiac launches rebellion against British.

1786 Tlingit on Northwest coast first encounter whites.

1804–06 Lewis and Clark lead expedition to Pacific Ocean.

1730   1740   1750   1760   1770   1780   1790   1800   1810   1820

1741 Russian ships start exploring Northwest coast.

1769 Spanish establish missions in California; over the next 60 years Native population of California declines due to disease and forced labor.

1791 Chief Little Turtle inflicts 900 casualties on U.S. forces; worst U.S. defeat in any war against the Indians.

1809–11 Tecumseh campaigns for American Indians to unify in opposition to the European conquest of their homeland.

1924 Indian Citizenship Act passed.

1934 Indian Reorganization Act passed, part of Roosevelt's New Deal for American Indians.

1969–71 Indian activists occupy Alcatraz Island.

1979 Seminole open 1,700-seat bingo parlor.

2004 National Museum of American Indian opens in Washington, D.C.

1920   1930   1940   1950   1960   1970   1980   1990   2000   2010

1941–45 25,000 Native Americans see active service with U.S. forces during World War II.

1953 U.S. Congress begins to implement Indian termination policy.

1973 Activists from American Indian Movement and local Oglala Sioux stage armed takeover of town of Wounded Knee.

2000 U.S. Census records 4,000,000 Americans who classify themselves as Native Americans.

The Coso petroglyphs located near China Lake, California, may be more than 10,000 years old.

CHAPTER 1
THE BEGINNING

The first people arrive in North America

At the beginning of the last Ice Age, there were no humans anywhere in North America. By the time Europeans arrived in the 16th century, the continent was home to a dazzling array of societies, from the mighty Aztec Empire in present-day Mexico, to the bison hunters of the Great Plains, to the resourceful Inuit peoples of the North. Where did all these people come from? How did they develop into such a diverse collection of tribes and cultures? This chapter follows the path of the ancient hunter-gatherers who first crossed the Bering Land Bridge more than 10,000 years ago, and tracks the gradual changes that led to the formation of the Indian and Mesoamerican cultures whose legacies lives on today.

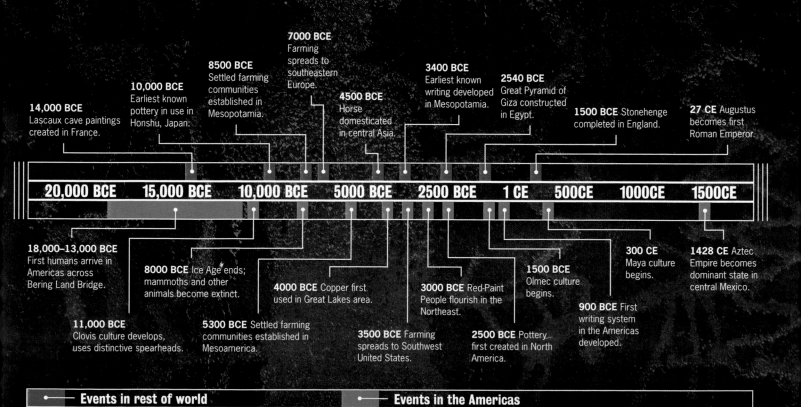

7000 BCE Farming spreads to southeastern Europe.

8500 BCE Settled farming communities established in Mesopotamia.

3400 BCE Earliest known writing developed in Mesopotamia.

2540 BCE Great Pyramid of Giza constructed in Egypt.

10,000 BCE Earliest known pottery in use in Honshu, Japan.

4500 BCE Horse domesticated in central Asia.

14,000 BCE Lascaux cave paintings created in France.

1500 BCE Stonehenge completed in England.

27 CE Augustus becomes first Roman Emperor.

| 20,000 BCE | 15,000 BCE | 10,000 BCE | 5000 BCE | 2500 BCE | 1 CE | 500CE | 1000CE | 1500CE |

18,000–13,000 BCE First humans arrive in Americas across Bering Land Bridge.

8000 BCE Ice Age ends; mammoths and other animals become extinct.

4000 BCE Copper first used in Great Lakes area.

3000 BCE Red-Paint People flourish in the Northeast.

1500 BCE Olmec culture begins.

300 CE Maya culture begins.

1428 CE Aztec Empire becomes dominant state in central Mexico.

11,000 BCE Clovis culture develops, uses distinctive spearheads.

5300 BCE Settled farming communities established in Mesoamerica.

3500 BCE Farming spreads to Southwest United States.

2500 BCE Pottery first created in North America.

900 BCE First writing system in the Americas developed.

● Events in rest of world   ● Events in the Americas

THE ICE AGE AND THE LAND BRIDGE

The first people to arrive in North America didn't realize they were traveling to a new continent—they were only following their food supply. Nevertheless, their journey paved the way for thousands of years of Native American cultures.

THE LAND BRIDGE

During the last Ice Age—which ended about 10,000 years ago—much of the earth's water was locked up in huge blocks of ice called glaciers. This lowered ocean levels and exposed a bridge of land across the Bering Strait, connecting Alaska and Siberia. Estimates of this land bridge's width range from 200 miles (322 km) up to 1,000 miles (1,609 km). It was a cold land of barren tundra, but unlike many northern regions, it was not covered by glacial ice.

In prehistoric times, groups of hunting families wandered across the land bridge from Asia to America without realizing where they were going. They were simply following the mammals they depended on for food, such as the caribou and the imposing woolly mammoth. On occasion, groups of people probably moved back to the west, but in general the animals were moving to the east, from Asia to North America, and the ancient hunters followed.

Glaciers once covered a large portion of North America. Today, their coverage has been much reduced.

The last to cross the land bridge were the ancestors of the Inuit and Aleuts, who now inhabit the frozen lands of Alaska and northern Canada.

Over the course of many centuries, the first people migrated to North America, then spread south and east, taking whatever routes they could find through the huge glaciers that covered the continent's northern half. Eventually, some migrants crossed another narrow strip of land, corresponding to modern Central America. They then fanned out through South America, until the entire region of the Americas was populated by human beings.

OTHER THEORIES

Over the years, some scholars have developed theories that ancient inhabitants of the Americas reached the area in other ways, such as sailing to South America from the Polynesian islands of the western Pacific, or walking across

KEY

Ice cap during Wisconsin glaciation (land/sea)

Bering Strait land bridge

Possible migration routes of early Indians

This map shows the routes the first people took as they populated North and Central America, as well as the extent of the glaciers during the Ice Age.

The first people in America hunted caribou and mammoths.

The people who crossed the Bering Strait during the Ice Age used spears to hunt a wide variety of game.

HE'S NOT THAT BIG!

Woolly mammoths were about the size of modern elephants, but had much longer tusks.

a different land bridge that linked northern Europe to Greenland. While these theories are intriguing, there is no direct evidence to support them, and most scholars continue to regard the Bering Land Bridge as the only—or, at the very least, the primary—route of migration.

FACTS AND FIGURES

One of the exciting things about the history of ancient America is that it is so fluid, constantly changing as new evidence is discovered. For example, most scientists feel that the first people to arrive probably came 15,000 to 20,000 years ago, but some researchers feel that the time frame might reach back as far as 40,000 years.

In addition, there is no clear agreement on how many people were living in the Americas at the time of Columbus's voyage in 1492. (In part, this is due to a lack of consensus over how many Native people died from European diseases in the centuries after the first contact.) Several scholars have estimated the population at around 12.5 million north of the Rio Grande and 100 million for the entire hemisphere. Other scientists, however, find these figures far too high. They estimate that there were no more than two million people living in all of North America. The regional population figures given in this book are based on a total of about 2.6 million, closer to the lower end of the spectrum.

ADAPTING TO THE ENVIRONMENT

As the glaciers melted and retreated toward the North Pole, the North American environment changed slowly—but in dramatic ways. Over time, the basic landforms and climate regions of today emerged. During this period, the Native people of America developed hunting and farming skills that laid the groundwork for the cultures to come.

NEW TECHNOLOGIES

About 13,000 years ago, America's first inhabitants started adapting to their environment in increasingly inventive ways. They began using workable stone, such as flint, chert, and obsidian to make knives and spear points. Having no metal tools, they carved these stones with antler or bone, using a technique called "pressure flaking" to press flakes or chips off the stone. The earliest spear points in North America date from around 11,000 BCE, and are associated with a society known as the Clovis culture. About 2,000 years later, a group known as the Folsom culture flourished, making their own distinctive points.

THE AGRICULTURAL REVOLUTION

Researchers have been surprised to discover that some groups in America developed limited farming as early as 8000 BCE. Combined with hunting and gathering wild plants, farming provided these groups with a more reliable food supply, allowing them to abandon the nomadic lifestyle and live in settled villages.

Corn was first domesticated in the hills of Mexico about 7,000 years ago. It was bred from a wild grass called teosinte, and the first cobs were about the size of a thumbnail. Over several centuries, plants with larger cobs were developed, in hundreds of different varieties. From Mexico, the techniques of corn cultivation spread both south and north, and corn soon became the staple food of many Indian societies. It was easy to grow, as long as birds were kept away—a task that usually fell to the children. Many varieties of beans were also domesticated, as well as squashes and melons.

In addition to leading toward the establishment of permanent settlements, the more reliable food supply also meant that many areas could support more people, leading to an increase in the density of the population.

CLOVIS POINT

FOLSOM POINT

These spear points show the distinctive shapes associated with the Clovis and Folsom cultures. For clarity, they are shown larger than life.

Wherever corn became an important crop, it also acquired a spiritual significance. Many later Indian societies associated corn with the origin of life and incorporated the crop into their myths about creation. For example, the Omaha Indians on the eastern Great Plains "sang up" the corn in a special ritual to encourage its growth. To the north, the Mandan had a corn priest, who presided over ceremonies during the growing season. And among the Zuni, who lived in the arid environment of the Southwest, each infant was given an ear of corn at birth, which served as a "corn mother."

As farming spread throughout North America, certain techniques and combinations of crops enjoyed widespread popularity. One common strategy involved growing three crops together—corn, beans, and squash. Within a small area, bean vines were planted to climb up the corn stalk and

game over a cliff took a great deal of cooperation.

Spears were the primary hunting weapon and the Indians traveled on foot. Early societies occasionally used fire during hunts to drive animals into a canyon or a makeshift corral. Experts recognize that many Native societies also used fire to modify their environment in certain ways, such as clearing part of a forest to create more grazing land for deer or other animals.

STARTING TO DIVERSIFY

As people spread throughout North America and began settling in permanent villages, different groups began developing their own

The three sisters (corn, beans, and squash) were a hallmark of early agriculture in North America. Today, this would be considered a form of "companion planting."

individual practices. Starting out as simple adaptations to the continent's different environments, these customs would eventually blossom into a rich variety of distinctive societies and cultures.

Some groups in America developed farming as early as 8000 BCE.

squash grew along the ground, keeping the soil cool and holding in moisture. This combination became known as the "three sisters," and was important in the cultures of many North American tribes.

HUNTING IN GROUPS

Even as farming took hold across the continent, early Indian societies continued to rely heavily on hunting. For some groups, hunting and gathering wild foods were still the only ways of acquiring food. In fact, a few societies never developed agriculture at all.

Hunting was almost always a group activity. Often, Indians hunted in family units, and women were frequently involved. Tasks such as flushing animals out of a thicket or herding large

I HOPE THOSE SPEAR POINTS AREN'T ACTUAL SIZE.

Elk were an important food source for early people in many parts of North America.

INCREASING DIVERSITY

The various environmental regions of North America challenged America's first people in different ways and provided a wide range of possible lifestyles. Within each Indian society, one generation after another gradually changed its habits according to the surroundings. Some groups moved when their food supplies ran out. Others found new sources or techniques.

Copper tools and ornaments, such as these, were made by a culture in the Great Lakes region starting around 4000 BCE. At the time, they were the only people in North America to make objects out of metal.

THE RED-PAINT PEOPLE

Depending on the environment and the raw materials available, early North American societies developed their own unique skills and arsenals of tools and weapons. For example, from 3000 to 500 BCE, a group known as the Red-Paint People lived in New England and eastern Canada. Modern researchers have given them this name because of their prominent use of ground-up red hematite, a form of iron oxide, to decorate their bodies and crafts.

Burial sites associated with this culture have revealed beautifully made tools, figurines, and various decorative objects made from bone, quartzite, slate, and antler. The Red-Paint People even created fire-making kits containing flints and pyrite.

THE GREAT LAKES REGION

Like their neighbors in the Northeast, the early people in the Great Lakes region lived in clearings surrounded by thick forests. They too used a variety of materials to make ornaments and tools, including wood, bone, stone, antlers, and shells.

Starting around 4000 BCE, the people of the Great Lakes region also used copper, making them unique among the early inhabitants of North America. On the southern shore of Lake Superior, they found nuggets and rough pieces of the metal. At first they worked it like stone by chipping off pieces to shape tools and rough ornaments. In time, however, they learned to smelt the copper by heating and then cooling it. This enabled them to make extraordinary objects that were also very durable.

Soon, copper items became extremely valuable. Demand led to widespread trade with neighboring cultures, which in turn brought a greater variety of goods to the people of the Great Lakes.

THE GREAT BASIN

The Great Basin (see pp.50–51) is a bowl-shaped region surrounded by mountains, in present-day Utah and Nevada. Although the area once contained dozens of lakes, most of them disappeared over time. At the southern extreme is the desert known as Death Valley, where summer highs range from 120 to 140°F (49 to 60°C).

This is not a human-friendly environment, yet people have lived here for centuries by hunting small animals and gathering whatever plants they can find. One way the early residents of the Great Basin met the challenge of their environment was by producing baskets—in fact, they were the first people in North America to do so. These baskets had a variety of uses, including holding water and cooking food. Great Basin peoples also made twine out of hair, fur, and plant fibers. This twine was used to make traps for small animals.

Over time, these ancient societies evolved into the Indian cultures we know today.

This coiled basket made by the Washo tribe of the Great Basin is similar to those made by the region's earlier inhabitants.

OTHER EXAMPLES OF EARLY INVENTIVENESS

There are many other examples of the early people of the Americas displaying great creativity in adapting to their environment. Some tribes devised new methods for preparing, preserving, and storing food. One widely copied system involved heating stones and dropping them in a pit or container to cook stews or other food. In addition to baskets, many groups designed containers made from animal skins for storing food or water.

Between 5000 and 500 BCE, different groups of early Americans devised a wide variety of tools and weapons. These included spears, knives, axes, hammers, anvils, mortars and pestles, fish hooks, harpoons, and tobacco pipes. Special tools were needed to shape logs into dugout canoes, such as awls, drills, mauls, and scrapers. For hunting, a number of tribes developed a device called an *atlatl*, which they used to launch spears with much greater thrust and distance than could be achieved when they were thrown by hand.

In later centuries, the first people of North America also displayed great creativity in building dwellings, making use of the materials the environment offered to construct a wide variety of homes. The names of these dwellings give an idea of their diversity—they included tipis, longhouses, pit houses, hogans, wigwams, wickiups, igloos, earth lodges, chickees, pueblos, lean-tos, and more.

When ancient people started living in permanent villages, they ended up supplying modern archeologists with a great deal of evidence in the form of refuse heaps known

An atlatl was a device used to throw spears with greater force than could be achieved when they were thrown by hand.

as middens. In coastal areas, enormous oyster shell middens have been uncovered—on some islands in Georgia, middens have been found that are more than 9 feet (2.7 m) high and 300 feet (91 m) in diameter. These middens provide important insights into the early people of North America, telling us about what they ate and how they lived their lives. As these ancient societies continued to diversify, they evolved into the Indian cultures that we know today.

A shell midden is already being formed in this ancient North American camp.

OLMEC AND MAYA

This book deals chiefly with the inhabitants of North America north of the Rio Grande, in what is now the United States and Canada. However, to the south, in Mesoamerica (Mexico and Central America), three great civilizations flourished in the centuries before European contact: the Olmec, the Maya, and the Aztec. To varying degrees, all three of these societies had important influences on their neighbors to the north.

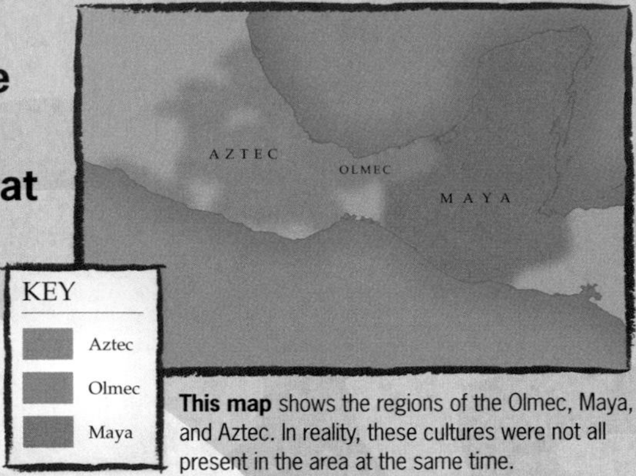

KEY

- Aztec
- Olmec
- Maya

This map shows the regions of the Olmec, Maya, and Aztec. In reality, these cultures were not all present in the area at the same time.

TALK ABOUT A BIG HEAD!

OLMEC INNOVATIONS

Agriculture was key to the development of the first advanced civilizations. As farming techniques developed, the people of present-day Mexico began growing surpluses of corn and other crops. This allowed some people to indulge in other pursuits, such as crafts and trade. One of the first societies to capitalize on food surpluses in this way were the Olmec. Active from 1500 to 300 BCE, the Olmec developed a number of religious and economic centers in southern Mexico. Their achievements included the development of a calendar and one of the world's first systems of writing. They built towering pyramids, as well as massive stone heads that are now famous throughout the world.

The stone heads carved by the Olmec weighed up to 20 tons (18 metric tons).

MAYAN CIVILIZATION

Building on the achievements of the Olmec and other early cultures, the Maya developed a remarkable civilization in the Yucatán Peninsula and the highlands of Mexico. Like the Olmec, the Maya followed a way of life based around religious centers. Researchers have found 116 such sites in Mexico and Central America. These centers were home to a variety of impressive stone structures, including pyramids, temples, platforms for astronomical observations, palaces, and monasteries. There were also plazas, ball courts, aqueducts, and reservoirs. Tikal, the largest of the Mayan centers, had 3,000 structures and an estimated population of 30,000 to 60,000 people.

Mayan priests were the keepers of knowledge, and the custodians of the calendars. Craftspeople, such as jewelers and stonemasons, were also prominent members of society. Clothing designers made elaborate garments for members of royal households, using cotton, gold thread, and feathers.

TRADE TIES WITH THE NORTH

The Maya established trade routes over wide areas, stretching both north and south. Merchants traveled considerable distances in large dugout canoes powered by as many as 20 paddlers. Corn and other agricultural products found their way to the Southwest and Gulf Coast areas of the modern United States. In exchange, trade items from the north, such as turquoise and exotic feathers, may have found their way to the Maya.

MAYAN ACHIEVEMENTS

At their peak, from 600 to 900 CE, the Maya dominated much of what is now central Mexico, Guatemala, and Belize. They adapted to many environments, from lowlands to rain forests. Mayan astronomers calculated solar and lunar eclipses with great precision. In fact, their calendar was more accurate than the one we use today.

The Mayan calendar was more accurate than the one we use today.

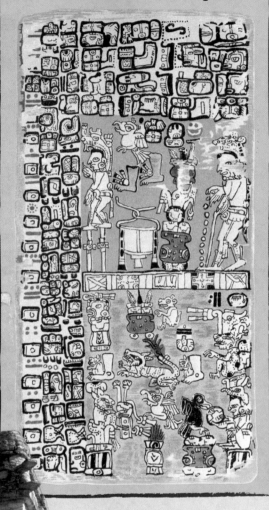

The Mayan Calendar

The Mayan calendar reaches back to August 11, 3114 BCE, which coincides with the building of the early pyramids in ancient Egypt. It ends in 2012, but starts again right away, introducing a new, long epoch of several centuries called a "Long Count."

The Temple of the Seven Dolls, named after seven small sculptures found there, is located at the Maya site of Dzibilchaltún, in Mexico. During the spring equinox, the rising sun shines exactly through one window of the temple and out the other.

The Pyramid of the Magician is the central structure of the ancient Maya city of Uxmal, in Yucatán, Mexico.

THE AZTEC AND THEIR CONQUEST

REPRODUCTION OF AZTEC SUN STONE

The Aztec Empire was the last of the great Mesoamerican civilizations. Building on the achievements of earlier societies, the Aztec created many impressive structures and beautiful art objects. In 1519, the empire was in full flower when it was invaded by the Spanish. This invasion was the first large-scale conquest of an American civilization by a European power, setting a precedent for events north of the Rio Grande.

AZTEC CULTURE

There were many small societies in the Valley of Mexico when the Aztec moved in from the north around 1248. Perhaps because of crowding, they settled on the

Tenochtitlan was a city of nearly 300,000 people at the heart of the Aztec Empire, as depicted in this Mexico City mural.

islands of Lake Texcoco. To create more space they developed structures called *chinampas*—artificial islands made of large wicker baskets, anchored to the shallow bottom of the lake and filled with silt and plant matter. More land was acquired by draining swamps on the edge of the lake.

On the reclaimed land, the Aztec built Tenochtitlan, which they called the "City of

the Gods." Today's Mexico City occupies the same area. Tenochtitlan consisted of hundreds of buildings, painted in a rainbow of colors—red, yellow, green, and turquoise. The population is estimated to have been close to 300,000. At the peak of the Aztec's power, the city was the capital of a widespread empire, built through trade and military conquest.

An **Aztec priest** offers a living person's heart to the war god Huitzilopochtli, in a vivid example of human sacrifice.

HUMAN SACRIFICE

Like other Mesoamerican cultures, the Aztec engaged in the practice of human sacrifice as part of their religion. In fact, they took the practice to extremes that we would now consider horrifying. Based on the number of skulls found at the Great Temple at the time of the Spanish invasion, it is estimated that 10,000 to 60,000 people had been sacrificed there in the 32 years since its construction. The public displays of sacrifices sometimes involved killing four people at a time, at several times throughout the day. Often, a priest tore the hearts out of the victims.

THE SPANISH CONQUEST

The Spanish conquest of the Aztec Empire would have an enormous influence on the peoples of North America. Following the accidental "discovery" of the Americas by Christopher Columbus in 1492, the Spanish showed little interest in the area. Then, in 1519, a Spanish conquistador named Hernán Cortés landed on the coast of Mexico with a force of about 400 men. He made alliances with several kingdoms whose rulers were bitter enemies of the Aztec. Over the next two years, using trickery as well as alliances, Cortés conquered the Aztec Empire, destroyed their magnificent capital city, and took thousands of Aztec lives.

The Spanish had several advantages that helped them achieve victory over the Aztec people. In the beginning, the Aztec were frightened by the Spanish horses, having never seen such animals before. In addition, Spanish weapons such as the crossbow could kill at greater distances than those of the Native people. Most devastating of all were the European diseases such as smallpox that the Spanish brought with them. The Aztec's bodies had no natural defenses against these illnesses, and they succumbed to them in

Montezuma, ruler of the Aztec Empire, was eventually held hostage in his own palace by the Spanish. In this 16th-century painting, he begs his people to surrender, though it is not clear this actually occurred.

huge numbers. Later, Native peoples across North and South America would be similarly ravaged by European diseases.

During the period of Spanish conquest, deaths from war, forced labor, and disease decimated the Aztec people. The population of what is now Mexico declined from more than 18 million in 1520 to less than 2 million in 1650. This was the greatest population loss in human history.

THE IMPACT ON NORTH AMERICA

Throughout the 1500s, ships loaded with plundered treasure sailed from the Americas to Spain, quickly making Spain the wealthiest nation in the world—and the envy of Europe's other kingdoms. In the 1530s, Francisco Pizarro conquered the great Inca Empire in South America, sending still more treasure to Spain.

Other Spanish conquistadors turned to the north, exploring the edges of North America, and even the interior, in Florida and the Southwest. Soon, explorers from other European countries probed farther north, hoping to repeat the Spanish success. Some searched for a Northwest Passage—a water route through or around North America that would serve as a shortcut to the riches of Asia. Others traded with the Indians for animal furs. By 1600, a growing number of European groups and nations were looking for ways to establish colonies in the New World.

These early incursions were the opening chapters in the European conquest of North America and its people. Over the coming centuries, the devastation suffered by the Aztec would be experienced in different forms by the Indian tribes and nations to the north.

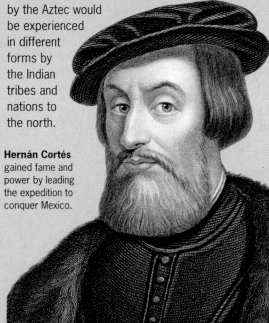

Hernán Cortés gained fame and power by leading the expedition to conquer Mexico.

This Blackfoot shield is made from buffalo hide, a common material among the tribes of the Great Plains.

CHAPTER 2

THE EMERGENCE OF INDIAN CULTURES

Tribes develop distinctive ways of life

Before the arrival of Europeans, there were millions of people living in the present-day United States and Canada. Depending on their culture and environment, these people lived in many different ways. In the arid desert of the Great Basin, they dug through the soil in search of anything edible. On the Plateau, they brought in huge hauls of fish under the guidance of a salmon chief. This chapter looks at the wide variety of tribes in pre-contact North America, from the Pueblo villages of the Southwest to the portable tipi camps of the Great Plains.

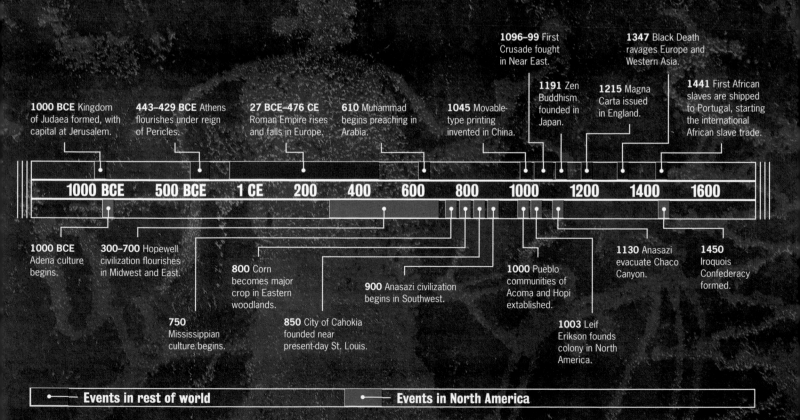

1096–99 First Crusade fought in Near East.

1347 Black Death ravages Europe and Western Asia.

1191 Zen Buddhism founded in Japan.

1215 Magna Carta issued in England.

1441 First African slaves are shipped to Portugal, starting the international African slave trade.

1000 BCE Kingdom of Judaea formed, with capital at Jerusalem.

443–429 BCE Athens flourishes under reign of Pericles.

27 BCE–476 CE Roman Empire rises and falls in Europe.

610 Muhammad begins preaching in Arabia.

1045 Movable-type printing invented in China.

| 1000 BCE | 500 BCE | 1 CE | 200 | 400 | 600 | 800 | 1000 | 1200 | 1400 | 1600 |

1000 BCE Adena culture begins.

300–700 Hopewell civilization flourishes in Midwest and East.

800 Corn becomes major crop in Eastern woodlands.

900 Anasazi civilization begins in Southwest.

1000 Pueblo communities of Acoma and Hopi established.

1130 Anasazi evacuate Chaco Canyon.

1450 Iroquois Confederacy formed.

750 Mississippian culture begins.

850 City of Cahokia founded near present-day St. Louis.

1003 Leif Erikson founds colony in North America.

— **Events in rest of world**

— **Events in North America**

THE MOUND-BUILDING CULTURES

Before the familiar regional cultures that were present at the time of European contact, the eastern half of North America was home to a series of societies known for building large earthen mounds. When Europeans discovered these mounds, they were puzzled, theorizing that they must have been built by ancient Egyptians or other Europeans. Over the past 50 years, a clearer picture of these early societies has finally begun to emerge.

ADENA CULTURE (1000 BCE–200 CE)

Named after an estate in Ohio, the Adena culture occupied parts of present-day Ohio, Kentucky, and West Virginia. Members of this society grew only a few crops, but the forests and waterways provided ample food to support large villages. They used pottery and copper tools imported from the Great Lakes region, and they also made cloth from vegetable fibers.

Around 1000 BCE, the Adena became the first to build burial mounds, as well as larger mounds for ceremonial purposes.

The most famous of the Adena constructions is the "Serpent Mound," which coils for a quarter mile (.4 km) along a river near present-day Cincinnati, Ohio. The mounds indicate the presence of highly developed social and religious structures, since a central authority would be needed to supervise their construction. Additionally, most mounds served as burial chambers, and placing materials in the chambers required considerable time and effort.

Little is known of the daily life of the Adena settlements or the nature of their religious beliefs and practices. Even less is known about why the culture vanished. Some researchers believe that a change in climate may have forced them to move and to change their way of life.

HOPEWELL CULTURE (300 BCE–700 CE)

The Hopewell culture was similar to the Adena in many ways, but was characterized by richer burials, more complex rituals, larger mound structures, and a greater reliance on farming. It also covered a much larger area, from its core in the Ohio and Illinois river valleys to much of the Midwest and East. The Hopewell also traded over a wide area. Obsidian from the Rocky Mountains, shells from the Gulf Coast, and silver from Canada have all been found within their mounds.

The Hopewell seem to have been governed by priest-rulers. Their villages, usually located near waterways, were made up of round, dome-roofed wigwams, covered with sheets of bark or woven plant fibers. Many of their mounds were more than 30 feet (9 m) high, enclosed by earthen walls that were even higher, and often 200 feet (61 m) wide at the base. Hopewell craftspeople were highly skilled. Archeological digs have uncovered copper headdresses, pearl necklaces, obsidian knives and spearheads, clay figurines, and sculptures of humans and animals.

So far, researchers have not learned where the Hopewell people came from. And little is known about why they vanished sometime around 700 CE. Theories range from crop failure, to epidemics, to war. The only certain thing is that other mound builders followed in their wake.

This Hopewell hand was cut from a sheet of mica rock. Experts are uncertain as to how this object was used.

The Great Serpent Mound was created by the Adena culture in present-day Ohio. It is 1,330 feet (405 m) long and consists of three separate sections.

had connections with Mesoamerican civilizations (see pp.22–27), but so far no direct evidence has been found. Indications of a connection are found in the Mississippians' preoccupation with death, and in evidence of human sacrifice, both of which are common features of Mesoamerican culture.

By the early 1600s, the great Mississippian centers had been abandoned and, again, there is no clear evidence of why. One later culture that retained many of the Mississippian traits was that of the Natchez Indians, who were absorbed into other Indian societies after a series of conflicts with the French in the 1700s (see p.68). Meanwhile, during much of the mound-culture period, other Indian groups were developing cultures that are considerably less mysterious.

MISSISSIPPIAN CULTURE (700–1600 CE)

Centered in the Southeast, the Mississippian culture spread as far north as Wisconsin. The people farmed the Mississippi River

Located near the present-day city of St. Louis, Cahokia contains the ruins of a 10-story ceremonial mound known as Monk's Mound that covered some 15 acres. The city itself, laid out over six square miles (16 sq km), also contained 120 smaller mounds, which had various

Copper animal effigies, like this pair of frogs, were placed in burial mounds by the Hopewell people.

By the early 1600s, the great Mississippian centers had been abandoned.

Valley, growing huge crops of corn, beans, squash, melons, and tobacco. They also hunted, fished, and gathered wild foods.

With population estimates running from 8,000 to 40,000, Cahokia was by far the largest Mississippian mound center. Established about 1000 CE, it was also one of the most recent.

practical and ceremonial purposes.

In all the Mississippian villages, the people lived in small houses with thatched roofs, built in neat rows. Researchers strongly suspect that the mound cultures

Cahokia was a bustling community, with the 100-foot (30 m) Monk's Mound at the center.

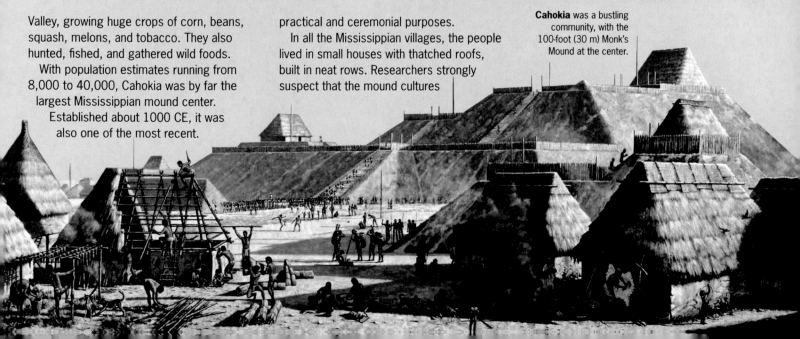

MONK'S MOUND

The earthwork known as Monk's Mound was the center of the Mississippian settlement of Cahokia, which was established around 1000 CE near present-day St. Louis. Constructed almost entirely of earth, the mound is more than 100 feet (30 m) high, and is the largest manmade earth mound in North America.

Trees would have been cut down to make way for the 90-acre community plaza.

Concrete stairway follows approximate path of ancient wooden steps to top of mound.

Landscape was probably artificially leveled by Mississippian workers.

Base of mound takes up 16 acres, more than the base of the Great Pyramid of Giza in Egypt.

THE SOUTHWEST

The Southwest is a land of stunning beauty, from the mesas of the Colorado Plateau to the hardened dunes of the Painted Desert. Before European contact, this varied environment was home to a series of advanced societies, some of which still exist in the area today.

FARMING IN A DRY AND RUGGED LAND

Most Southwest cultures relied heavily on farming. In fact, nowhere else in North America was agriculture so highly developed, even though the environment is not inviting to the practice. The region is remarkably dry, with precipitation less than 20 inches (51 cm) a year and less than 5 inches (13 cm) in some areas. However, that dryness is actually one of the reasons the people turned to farming, since the climate meant that only limited resources were available from hunting and gathering. In addition, the rugged landscape allowed farming societies to build their villages in areas that offered some protection from raids by nomadic tribes.

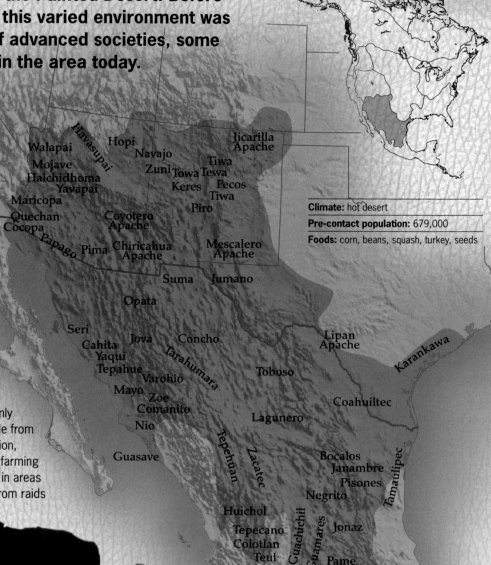

Climate: hot desert

Pre-contact population: 679,000

Foods: corn, beans, squash, turkey, seeds

Walapai
Havasupai
Hopi
Navajo
Jicarilla Apache
Mojave
Zuni
Tiwa
Towa Tewa
Halchidhoma
Yavapai
Keres
Pecos
Tiwa
Maricopa
Coyotero Apache
Piro
Quechan
Cocopa
Papago
Pima
Chiricahua Apache
Mescalero Apache
Suma
Jumano
Opata
Seri
Jova
Concho
Lipan Apache
Karankawa
Cahita
Yaqui
Tarahumara
Toboso
Tepahue
Varohio
Coahuiltec
Mayo
Zoe
Comanito
Lagunero
Nio
Tepehuan
Zacatec
Bocalos
Janambre
Pisones
Tamaulipec
Guasave
Negrito
Huichol
Guachichil
Guamares
Jonaz
Tepecano
Colotlan
Teul
Pame

POTTERY OF ALL KINDS

Many of the Southwest people were (and are) excellent potters. The Pueblo people in particular were known for making clay vessels adorned with striking geometric designs, as were their ancestors, known as the Ancestral Pueblo or Anasazi.

This Zuni bowl is decorated with frogs, and belonged to a rain priest. The Zuni are one of the Pueblo peoples.

This Apache doll helped initiate girls of the tribe into the world of adulthood.

THE PIMA AND THE PAPAGO

Of all the Southwest environments, none was more severe than that of the Pima and their relatives, the Papago. (Today, these tribes call themselves the Akimel O'odham and the Tohono O'odham.) The Pima lived near the area's few rivers, and the Papago's land, along the present-day Mexican border, was even drier. Both tribes disliked war, but could be effective fighters when necessary. The ceremonies of both tribes often included mock battles.

This Papago shield was used in mock battles. It is made of wood, painted hide, and feathers.

VILLAGERS AND NOMADS

Most of the Southwest tribes lived in settled villages. The Pueblo, for example, lived in distinctive adobe settlements that can still be seen today. However, after about 1400 CE, the area was also home to the semi-nomadic Apache tribes, who moved frequently and depended on hunting and gathering. There was often conflict between the two groups, as the Apache encroached upon Pueblo land and raided their villages. Eventually, the Navajo, who were descendants of the Apache, ended up adopting many Pueblo customs, including a more agricultural lifestyle.

Monument Valley is one of the Southwest's many breathtaking landscapes. The two buttes on the left are called the Mittens.

Before the emergence of familiar Southwest cultures such as the Pueblo and Navajo, several older societies flourished in the region. These peoples were fortunate to live near the advanced civilizations of Mesoamerica, which allowed them to develop an advanced lifestyle involving agriculture, irrigation, and pottery.

THE MOGOLLON CULTURE (100–1400 CE)

The rugged mountains along the border between present-day Arizona and New Mexico were home to a society known as the Mogollon. In addition to being excellent potters, the Mogollon were among the first in North America to adopt agriculture, probably acquiring the knowledge from Mesoamerican villages to the south. This technology enabled them to live in permanent villages. They built pit houses, about 4 feet (1.2 m) deep, with a frame of logs above and roofs made of branches and mud. These houses provided insulation against the desert's extreme temperature swings. By 1100, their villages had about 30 houses each, including one or more ceremonial centers or *kivas*. Between 1200 and 1400, the Mogollon culture faded, and its traits were absorbed by the Anasazi. Researchers believe that today's Zuni people are descendants of the Mogollon.

MOGOLLON POT

The Three Rivers Petroglyph Site in New Mexico contains a huge number of Mogollon petroglyphs, or rock carvings. Thought to have been created between 900 and 1400 CE, the carvings include images of birds, animals, humans, plants, and many abstract designs. With more than 21,000 carvings, it is one of the most abundant rock-art sites in the United States.

THE HOHOKAM CULTURE (200 BCE–1500 CE)

The Hohokam lived west of the Mogollons in the burning desert of the Gila River Valley. Like the Mogollon, they farmed, lived in pit houses, and were skilled potters. Their advanced irrigation systems included wide, shallow canals, some stretching for 10 miles (16 km), with valves made of woven mats. These systems made it possible for the Hohokam to build large settlements—the largest was Snaketown, near present-day Phoenix, Arizona, which they occupied for roughly 1,500 years. Many aspects of Hohokam art and culture were similar to that of the Mesoamericans to the south, suggesting a long-term interaction. Unlike their neighbors, however, the Hohokam were very peaceful; they did not share the Mesoamerican tradition of priest-rulers, forced payments to power centers, or aggression toward other societies. Around 1500, the Hohokam people abandoned their settlements and scattered into small groups. To this day, experts are not sure why.

HOHOKAM SHELL BRACELETS

ANASAZI CULTURE (100 BCE–1400 CE)

The Anasazi culture was centered in what is now known as the "Four Corners" region, where the states of Arizona, New Mexico, Utah, and Colorado intersect. The people were skilled in pottery and weaving, but they are best remembered for their housing. At first, the Anasazi lived in round, domed structures made of logs. These were later replaced by the pit houses used by the Mogollon and Hohokam. Then, sometime after 750 CE, they developed a style known as pueblo construction, whose influence can still be felt today. Pueblos were built entirely above ground, with walls of stone or adobe bricks and roofs of log beams. After a while, the Anaszai began to group several pueblo rooms together, with shared walls, and then began to put buildings on top of each other, connected by ladders. Nearby farms provided food for these large communities. Today, many experts prefer the term *Ancestral Pueblo* to *Anasazi*, since the modern Pueblo people are recognized to be direct descendants of the Anasazi. Many also include the Mogollon under this term.

Turquoise stones were a favorite material of Anasazi artisans. This frog is made of jet (a form of decayed wood), with turquoise on the eyes and neck. The frog was a symbol of water in Anasazi culture.

ANASAZI PITCHER

GOLDEN AGE AND DECLINE

The Anasazi enjoyed a Golden Age from about 1000 to 1300. A large population was spread over a wide area and supported many specialists, including potters, weavers, and builders. Cliff dwellings became popular during this period as an alternative to the pueblos. Then, around 1300, the Anasazi began abandoning their large settlements. Why did the Anasazi give up their great communities? As is often the case, there are no definite answers. It might have been a severe drought, invasion by nomadic tribes, or internal conflict. Whatever the cause, the Pueblo people were living in much smaller communities by the time Spanish explorers arrived.

Anasazi cliff dwellings, such as the Cliff Palace at Mesa Verde National Park, were built into the recesses of canyon walls.

THE NAVAJO

BEFORE EUROPEAN CONTACT

Around 1400, the Navajo's Apache ancestors migrated from the north into the arid lands near the home of the Pueblo people. The Pueblo lived in villages like their Anasazi ancestors, but the Navajo had always lived by hunting and gathering. Over time, the Navajo adopted many components of the agricultural lifestyle, living in settled communities and calling their new homeland *Dinetah,* meaning "land of the people." Although the Navajo are now associated with wool rugs and silver jewelry, these crafts were not developed until later, after contact with Europeans.

NAVAJO PITCHER

NAVAJO FAMILY VALUES

In Navajo culture, the family was the center of life, and the mother was the key figure. Girls were taught to tend the crops. They would also learn to prepare meals, preserve food, and make clothing and baskets. Boys, too, played an active role in the family's economy, performing daily chores such as hauling water, and helping to build new houses. A young couple's decision to marry was an occasion for great joy. The groom gave a gift, usually a deer, to the bride's family. During the marriage ceremony, the bride and groom washed each other's hands. A medicine man sprinkled corn pollen on them in two lines to symbolize the uniting of the two families. The family members ate a cornmeal porridge from each of the four sides of a woven basket. Finally, the medicine man advised the couple to seek help in keeping on the righteous path.

Wedding baskets were used in the Navajo marriage ceremony. Many were actually made by Paiute women, and then acquired by the Navajo through trade.

This Navajo woman is preparing traditional corn batter, surrounded by corncobs and husks. Although this photograph was taken in 1908, she is participating in a cultural practice that predates contact with Europeans by hundreds of years.

HOGANS AND HARMONY

Religion was central to almost every aspect of the Navajo's daily lives. Everything in the universe was meant to be in harmony, and people strove to achieve that balance by living the "good way." Even their traditional dwellings, called *hogans*, had to be built a certain way to conform to their beliefs. The blueprint of the hogan was said to have been created in the distant past by "First Man" and "First Woman." The door always faced east, toward the morning sun. When a new hogan was built, a singer led a ceremony to bring good fortune to the new home. Because the space was small, family members sat according to a set pattern: men sat against the south wall, women against the north. The children sat near their mother, and elders had a place of honor against the west wall.

Hogans were always built with the door facing east, toward the morning sun. Traditionally, a blanket was used to cover the entrance.

Sandpaintings lasted only one day, but today permanent versions are sometimes created for sale.

Yeibichai dancers performed during the Nightway ceremony, a Navajo chantway that was intended to restore harmomy.

BLESSINGWAYS AND CHANTWAYS

In Navajo culture, ceremonies known as *blessingways* were held for births, marriages, or any time someone needed good luck. When a person was sick, singers performed healing rituals known as *chantways*. During the chantway, a healer sprinkled colored sand or powders onto a deerskin or the level floor of a hogan, creating a detailed sandpainting following elaborate traditional designs. If the healing lasted more than a day, a new painting had to be created. Like many elements of Navajo culture, the concept of sandpaintings was originally borrowed from the Pueblo.

To see how the Navajo lived after contact with Europeans, see pp.102–103.

THE HOPI

The Hopi are one of the Pueblo peoples, a group of tribes that had many things in common, including their well-known adobe dwellings. Unlike many Native societies, the Hopi have largely preserved their culture into the modern age; all of the practices described here are still alive at the Hopi Reservation in Arizona.

LAND OF THE KACHINAS

Central to the Hopi religion, the spirits known as *kachinas* are said to visit their villages for a six-month period every year, usually starting in January. During this time, these messengers of the gods offer prayers for rain, a good harvest, and good health. There are about 250 different kachinas, which take the forms of birds, animals, plants, and humans. While the spirits are in town, men dressed as kachinas perform ritual dances. These include the Bean Dance, the Water Serpent Ceremony, and the Home Dance, which occurs when the kachinas return to the mountains in July.

PUEBLOS FOR THE PUEBLOS

The Hopi's villages are located in what is now northeastern Arizona. These villages, known as pueblos, are generally made up of a collection of multistoried buildings with apartment-like rooms, built on the tops of steep, flat hills called *mesas*. The dwellings are made of stone or mud-brick adobe in rectangular or circular shapes, and buildings occasionally overlook a central plaza. At the margins of the house blocks are structures known as *kivas*, which are built partially underground. Kivas are used for religious ceremonies and also house men's social clubs.

Kachina dolls are given to Hopi girls by the kachina dancers, while boys are given miniature bows and arrows. Today, the dolls are popular souvenirs, but some Hopi feel that imitation dolls are offensive to the kachina spirits.

Hopi villages consist of many multistoried buildings made of mud-brick adobe. The ancient village of Wàlpi, shown here, is located on top of a steep mesa in northern Arizona.

THE PEACEFUL ONES

One of the aspects of Hopi culture that is most admired today is the importance the tribe puts on peace. The Hopi believe that there were three worlds that existed before the present one, but they were destroyed because people had forgotten the teachings of the Great Spirit. They believe that humans are now living in the Fourth World, having emerged from the world below through a hole. A representation of this hole can be found at the bottom of every kiva. Because of this dramatic history, the Hopi are intent on living the right way by following the path of peace and by taking care of the environment. According to a Hopi prophecy, if humans fail to protect the environment, the world will be destroyed again in a "great purification." In fact, the Hopi environmental ethic was influential in the formation of the modern environmental movement in the United States.

The number four has great significance for the Hopi. For example, this illustration of a Hopi legend is divided into four sections, surrounded by four clouds. At the center is a symbol representing the Four Worlds: our current one and the three that came before it.

Hopi pottery makes use of striking geometric designs. It is usually "polychrome," featuring black and red patterns against a lighter background.

SNAKES AND RAIN

The Hopi enjoy elaborate ceremonies throughout the year. These ceremonies involve dances, poetry, songs, and recitations of ancient myths and legends. Many festivals are centered around rain and crops. Since the Hopi lands receive less than 10 inches (25 cm) of rain each year, the people do everything they can to ensure a healthy growing season. One particularly dramatic ceremony is known as the Snake Dance. In the time leading up to the dance, priests leave their villages to gather snakes, often taking young boys with them. On the day of the dance, the snakes are kept in a shrine known as a *kisi*. As the snake priests perform the dance, they remove snakes from the kisi and hold them in their hands, and even in their mouths! This ceremony is thought to bring rain, since snakes are associated with water.

The Hopi Snake Dance is performed by special snake priests, who hold live snakes in their hands and mouths. In this photograph, taken around 1899, a snake can be seen in the dancer's mouth as an excited crowd watches the performance.

THE GREAT PLAINS

The Great Plains is an area of grassland that stretches more than 2,000 miles (3,218 km) from present-day Canada south to Texas. It was home to Indian societies for at least 11,000 years before the first Europeans arrived. Over time, many of these tribes came to rely on the bison.

Sarcee
Plains Cree
Blood
Blackfoot
Piegan
Assiniboine
Plains Ojibwe
Gros Ventre
Hidatsa
Crow
Mandan
Yanktonai Sioux
Arikara
Santee Sioux
Shoshoni
Teton Sioux
Ponca
Yankton Sioux
Cheyenne
Omaha
Iowa
Pawnee
Oto
Arapaho
Ute
Kansa
Missouri
Osage
Jicarilla Apache
Kiowa
Kiowa-Apache
Quapaw
Apache
Comanche
Wichita
Caddo
Kitsai
Tawakoni
Tonkawa
Lipan Apache

Climate: grassland
Pre-contact population: 284,900
Foods: bison, corn, beans, squash

THE PLAINS ENVIRONMENT

The eastern Great Plains, where there is ample rainfall, have tall grasses. In the west, where there is half as much precipitation, the grasses are much shorter. There are a few stands of trees such as willow and cottonwood, but no large forests. While most of the region is quite flat, several hilly areas rise out of the prairie, including the Ozark Mountains and the Black Hills of South Dakota.

BLACK HILLS LANDSCAPE

Many Plains tribes used a *travois*, consisting of poles tied to either side of a dog, to transport materials.

SHAMANISM

In Plains societies, men were expected to undertake a vision quest, involving fasting and appeals to the spirit world for a guide, who usually took the form of an animal. Gifted individuals became shamans through their contacts with spirits. It was believed that shamans could tell the future and heal the sick.

This painted bison skull was used in the Blackfoot version of the Sun Dance.

WARFARE ON THE GREAT PLAINS

The Plains nations rarely fought large battles with heavy casualties. Instead, battles tended to be in the form of raids by small bands. Men fought for status and honor. Although battles could turn into bloody affairs, most Indians believed that the greatest exploit was to "count coup"—to touch an enemy and get away unharmed. The touch could be with a hand, a weapon, or a special "coup stick." A warrior could also win honor by rescuing a comrade. A successful warrior was received as a great hero.

Military societies, including "dog societies," were common in Plains tribes. In ceremonies, Hidatsa dog dancers always did the opposite of what they were told.

CHANGING WAYS OF LIVING

For many centuries, America's first people lived by hunting and gathering wild plants. Around 500 CE, farming led to a more reliable food supply, enabling many societies to live in semi-permanent villages, especially in the eastern Great Plains. These societies built their villages on the banks of rivers and streams. Around 1300, many of the eastern tribes, such as the Sioux and Comanche, moved west onto the flatter prairie to get away from larger tribes that were moving in from the east. On the prairie, Indian societies began a new, nomadic existence that depended on hunting bison. The bison provided them with most of the materials they needed to live. It was a thrilling, but often dangerous way of life.

Tomahawk pipes, such as this Dakota Sioux example, were used more as ceremonial objects than as weapons.

The Sioux were one of several Indian societies that moved west onto the Great Plains a few decades before the first contact with Europeans. In making the move, they gave up the regular food supply provided by farming, and took up the life of nomadic bison hunters. Experts now think they were probably forced to move because large tribes such as the Ojibwe were pressing them from the east.

HUNTERS AND BISON

As with other Plains tribes, a Sioux hunting party was made up of men, women, and children. The party had to move quite often to stay near the bison herds, and the usual hunting technique involved forcing a herd to stampede over a low cliff. Children waved blankets to stampede the bison. Men, often disguised as animals, then moved in close and drove the animals over the cliff. Women waited below, ready to move in quickly to skin and butcher the animals. One bison would provide a group with fresh meat for days, and dried meat, or jerky, lasted much longer.

Sioux hunters often wore animal skins as camouflage, as depicted in this painting by George Catlin.

A CEREMONIAL ANIMAL

Since the bison was so central to the Sioux way of life, it was only natural that pieces of the bison's body were often involved in Sioux rituals. Although the Sun Dance was the most important ceremony, there were many smaller rituals that were performed for special events and milestones in the lives of members of the tribe.

An Unwanted Name

Sioux is a shortened form of *Nadouessioux,* which was borrowed by Europeans from the language of the Odawa tribe. Although the term probably originally meant "speakers of a foreign language," some interpreted it to mean "small rattlesnake," and the Sioux people came to dislike it. However, because there is no replacement term that refers to all of the people in question, the word *Sioux* is used in this book.

A cradleboard was a convenient way to carry a Sioux baby.

A Sioux priest uses a bison skull and hide in a ritual intended to instill virtue in a child.

To see how the Sioux lived after contact with Europeans, see pp.96–97.

44

Preparing Bison Hides

1832 American artist George Catlin visited numerous Indian tribes. He knew that the Indian way of life would soon vanish and was eager to record as much as he could in art and writing. Here he describes how Sioux women tanned the hides of bison, which are also known as buffaloes.

In front of the tipis the women are seen busily at work, dressing robes and drying meat. The skindressing of the Indians, both of the buffalo and deerskins, is generally very beautiful and soft. Their mode of doing this is curious: they stretch the skin, either on a frame or on the ground, and after it has remained some three or four days with the brains of the buffalo or elk spread over the fleshy side, they grain it with a sort of adze or chisel, made of a piece of buffalo bone.

After the process of "graining," and the skin is apparently beautifully finished, they pass it through another process, that of "smoking." For this, a hole of some two or three feet in depth is dug in the ground, and a smothered fire kindled in the hole with rotten wood, producing a strong and peculiar sort of smoke; and over this a little tent, made of two or three buffalo-skins, and so closed as to prevent the smoke from escaping, in which the grained skins hang for three or four days. After this process, the dresses made of these skins may be worn repeatedly in the rain, and will always dry perfectly soft. . . .

JERKY AND PEMMICAN

When a bison was killed, the Sioux women moved in quickly to butcher the animal and, for a few days, everyone feasted on fresh meat. Because meat spoiled rapidly in the prairie heat, they saved the rest by cutting it into strips, which were dried in the sun to make jerky, a long-lasting trail food. Some of the jerky was cut into tiny pieces and mixed with berries, bison fat, and marrow to make pemmican, which would not spoil for many months, even years. Today, jerky and pemmican are both popular foods across the United States, among Indians and non-Indians alike.

Tanning bison hides was a complex process. Here, Sioux women prepare a hide while strips of jerky dry on a rack.

 # MADE FROM BISON

For Indians of the Great Plains, a bison was a raw-material warehouse. Its hide, horns, bones, fur, and even bladder were put to good use. Some items pictured here may have been made from non-bison products, but they are all similar to the types of objects the Plains tribes made from the bison.

CLOTHING

Belt
Belts or sashes were made from hide, and usually decorated with beadwork.

Moccasins
Moccasins made from hide were very tough.

Shirt
Hide was used in shirts. This one is from the Upper Missouri region.

Robe
This hide robe depicts warriors on horseback.

Headdress
Headdresses often had fur tassels at the sides.

Long moccasins
These tall moccasins helped protect the legs.

Bonnet
This Crow bonnet has real bison horns.

Bonnet
Bison horn bonnets were worn by members of warrior societies.

CHILDCARE

Cradle board
A Sioux baby spent much of its time in a hide bag on a wooden framework.

Doll
Children's dolls were made from a variety of material, including bison hide.

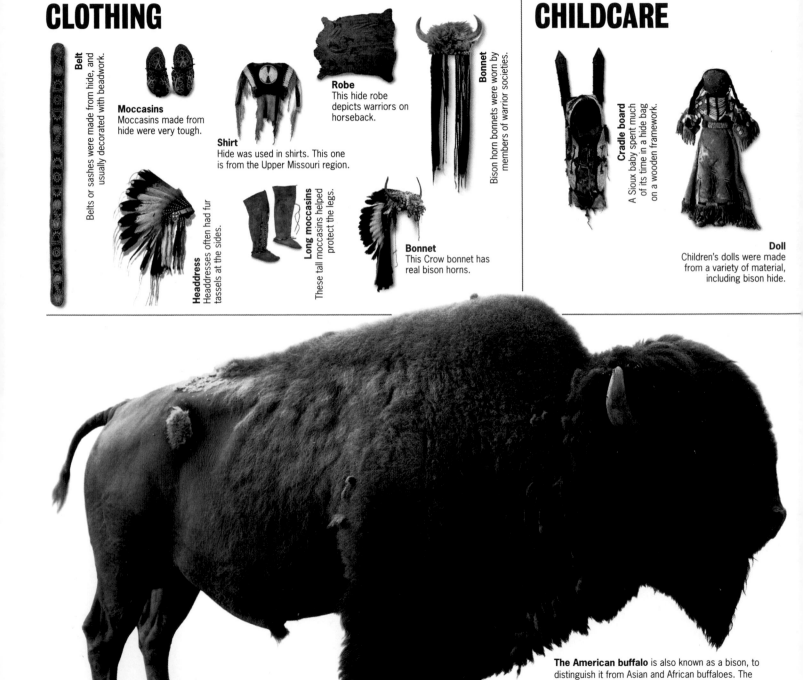

The American buffalo is also known as a bison, to distinguish it from Asian and African buffaloes. The largest native land mammal in the Americas, it was hunted nearly to extinction in the 19th century, but its population has since rebounded.

CONTAINERS

Pipe bag
Pipe bags were often heavily decorated.

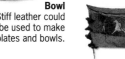

Storage bag
This Cheyenne storage bag is made from tanned bison hide.

Bowl
Stiff leather could be used to make plates and bowls.

Parfleche
These carry-alls were made from a single piece of rawhide.

Pouch
A bison's bladder could be made into a pouch.

Saddlebag
Plains riders hung these from saddles.

CEREMONIAL OBJECTS

Painted skull
This was placed on the altar during the Blackfoot Sun Dance.

Cupping horn
Bison horns were believed to draw out illness.

Ball
Balls made of hide were used in games such as shinny.

Rattle drum
Drums were used in many ceremonies.

Ceremonial case
This case was used to carry sacred objects during the Sun Dance.

Ghost dance wand
This Arapaho wand is wrapped in fur.

Drum
This drum was filled with water to give it a distinctive sound.

HORSERIDING

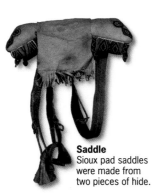

Saddle
Sioux pad saddles were made from two pieces of hide.

Rope
Women braided bison hair into ropes and lassos.

FOOD

Jerky
Dried bison meat could last for many months on the trail.

Fresh meat
Fresh bison meat was enjoyed for a few days after a kill.

WARFARE

Shield
This Blackfoot shield is made from neck hide, hardened by steam.

War club
This Sioux war club has a handle reinforced with rawhide.

SHELTER

Tipi
The hide walls of this dwelling were both practical and portable.

FUEL

Chips
Bison dung was used as fuel for fires.

TOOLS

Hammer
A stone and handle were covered in hide to make this tool.

Berry masher
Carved horn was used to make many practical utsensils.

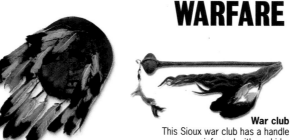

Utensils
These horn utensils were made in European style.

Hide scraper
Scrapers, used to smooth hides, were made from bone and teeth.

Flesher
Made from bone and teeth, fleshers scraped hair from hides.

Paintbrushes
These paintbrushes are made from pieces of bone.

Spoon
Carved horn spoons were used at feasts.

THE PLATEAU

The Plateau is a rugged, hilly area, laced with fast-moving rivers and flanked by the Cascade Mountains on the west, the Rockies on the east, and the Great Basin on the south. About two dozen Indian societies made their home in the region, including the Cayuse, Nez Perce, Columbia, and Klamath. Their ancestors had moved into the area before 6000 BCE.

Lillooet
Shuswap
Ntlakyapamuk
Nicola
Lake
Okanagan
Kootenai
Methow
Colville
Wenatchee
Sanpoil
Chelan
Kalispel
Chinook
Klickitat
Wanapam
Spokane
Coeur d'Alene
Yakima
Palouse
Walla Walla
Flathead
Wishram
Nez Perce
Tenino
Umatilla
Molala
Cayuse
Klamath
Modoc

Climate:	mountain forest, cool desert
Pre-contact population:	96,700
Food:	salmon, elk, deer, berries, bulbs

A deer figure made of rushes was used by the Ntlakyapamuk people in a ceremony to mark a death in the tribe.

CELEBRATIONS

The Plateau tribes held many ceremonies throughout the year. Among the Nez Perce, the month of May was called *Ah-Pah-Ahl*, meaning "the time for digging roots." Several tribes celebrated the Winter Dance, which lasted three days and was filled with stories, singing, and dancing. Often, residents of neighboring villages were invited. These shared celebrations strengthened tribal unity and made cold winters more enjoyable.

COLUMBIA RIVER GORGE

THE INFLUENCE OF GEOGRAPHY

The geography of an area doesn't determine how people must live, but it does present them with possibilities and limits. For example, some of the Plateau societies were fairly close to the bison herds of the Great Plains but not close enough to make bison hunting practical. However, the swift rivers of the Plateau were teeming with fish—sturgeon, trout, and most importantly, salmon, which was the staple of their diet. The rivers also served as highways for canoe travel.

FROM CHILD TO ADULT

As in other Indian societies, young people of the Plateau tribes were expected to undergo coming-of-age rituals. At the age of 12 or 13, a boy was sent on a vision quest. He was left on the top of a hill or mountain without food or weapons, in hope that he would experience a vision. In this vision, which often took the form of a dream, he would see his guardian spirit—an animal or a bird. Having seen his vision, he would return to his village and tell the council of elders what had happened. He was then welcomed into the tribe as an adult. If the youth did not have a vision, he was sent to try again. For girls, the coming-of-age ritual was different. She might spend a month away from the village, usually in a small lodge, accompanied by an older woman. Although she might have a vision, it wasn't required. She spent the last day in prayer and then returned to the village as a woman.

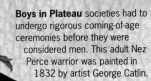

Boys in Plateau societies had to undergo rigorous coming-of-age ceremonies before they were considered men. This adult Nez Perce warrior was painted in 1832 by artist George Catlin.

A Wishram man spears salmon. The Wishram occupied a particularly salmon-rich stretch of the river called the Dalles.

SALMON AND OTHER FOODS

The Plateau societies established their villages in the sheltered river valleys, where they had easy access to salmon. The bountiful fish were caught using nets, basket traps, or three-pronged fishing spears. Most of the catch was dried on wooden racks, then stored in pits for winter use. Food for the day was soaked in oil and eaten raw, or else broiled on a stick. Every village had a wooded area for hunting deer and smaller game. Neighboring villages were often allowed to hunt there. Wild foods included berries and various roots.

Kettle Falls in Washington was a popular fishing site where many tribes converged. The enterprise was overseen by a "salmon chief."

THE GREAT BASIN

The harsh desert region known as the Great Basin does not offer a friendly environment for humans to live in. Nevertheless, several large Indian tribal groups had been living there for centuries at the time of the Europeans' first contact, including the Paiute, the Shoshoni, and the Ute. These tribes made the most of the region's minimal natural resources, and flourished despite the unforgiving nature of the land.

Northern Paiute (Paviotso)

Northern Shoshoni

Bannock

Eastern Shoshoni

Washo

Mono

Owens Valley

Panamint

Kawaiisu

Chemehuevi

Western Shoshoni

Gosiute

Ute

Southern Paiute

Climate: cool desert

Pre-contact population: 45,500

Foods: rabbits, snakes, insects, roots

Medicine Wheels

Some Great Basin tribes established large outdoor centers for religious ceremonies near rock formations. Rocks and boulders were used to form a ring known as a "medicine wheel," with spokes reaching out in many directions. Several of these rock structures, some measuring 80 feet (24 m) in diameter, are still visible throughout the area. It is believed they were used to mark sites for rituals or for vision quests.

The sandy plains in Utah's Great Salt Lake State Park are the remains of old lakes that have long since dried up.

A CHALLENGING ENVIRONMENT

As its name implies, the Great Basin is shaped like an enormous bowl, formed between mountains and uplands. It comprises virtually all of present-day Nevada and Utah, plus small portions of the surrounding states. Rivers and streams that flow in from the nearby high country drain into the basin, but there are no outlets to the ocean, so the water disappears into the ground in "sinks." In addition, few rainclouds can rise above the mountains to the east or west, so rainfall in the Great Basin is limited and evaporation is high. All told, this is one of the hottest, driest regions of the continent.

THE STRUGGLE TO SURVIVE

Because of the harshness of the Great Basin, the native people often used special sticks to dig for anything edible, including roots, snakes, and insects. They also hunted animals such as antelope, and sometimes fished. Small family groups spent nearly all their time searching for food, water, firewood, and raw materials. Because of such hardships, these Indians were nomads, rarely in one place for long. There were no villages and only limited tribal unity.

PRONGHORN ANTELOPE

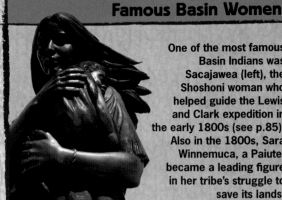

Famous Basin Women

One of the most famous Basin Indians was Sacajawea (left), the Shoshoni woman who helped guide the Lewis and Clark expedition in the early 1800s (see p.85). Also in the 1800s, Sara Winnemuca, a Paiute, became a leading figure in her tribe's struggle to save its lands.

SPECIAL CRAFTS

The objects created by the Basin Indians reflected their demanding environment. Shelter was often in caves or rock enclosures, but the people also built cone-shaped dwellings called *wickiups*. Clothing was minimal in the hot summer season. In colder weather, both men and women wore deerskin leggings and robes made of rabbit fur. The Basin tribes are also noteworthy for their distinctive basketry, which is both sturdy and beautiful. They were among the first on the continent to develop this craft, and many practitioners continued making them for sale through the 20th century. The baskets could be used to cook food, hold water, transport items, and trade for other goods. Some weavers traveled long distances in search of materials.

Newspaper Rock, in eastern Utah, contains one of the largest collections of petroglyphs in North America. The carvings were made by many tribes over a long period of time. It is thought that the earliest ones may date back more than 2,000 years.

Basket-making has long been an essential skill of the Basin tribes. Although this Paiute woman is dressed in European-influenced clothing, she is still engaged the ancient tribal craft of weaving plant matter into sturdy containers.

CALIFORNIA

At the time of first contact with Europeans, California was one of the most heavily populated regions north of Mexico, with population estimates running as high as 300,000. The people were divided into more than 100 cultural groups. Their villages were mostly scattered along a narrow coastal strip, hemmed in by mountains to the east. Although winter weather buries the northern mountains in heavy snow, most of the region enjoys a mild climate, which allowed an extraordinary wealth of people and cultures to flourish there.

Tolowa
Yurok Karok Shasta
Wiyot Hupa Achomawi
Wintun Atsugewi
Chimariko Yana
Nomlaki Yahi
Yuki Maidu
Pomo Konkow
Wappo Patwin
Miwok
Costano
Esselen
Mono
Salina Yokuts
Chumash
Tubatulabal
Kitanemuk
Serrano
Fernandeno
Gabrielino
Juaneno Cahuilla
Luiseno Cupeno
Diegueno
Kamia
Akwa'ala
Nakipa
Kiliwa
Cochimi
Ignacieno
Waicura
Pericu

Climate: hot desert, chaparral, forest
Pre-contact population: 287,300
Foods: acorns, berries, deer, rabbits, fish

MARIPOSA GROVE

A LAND OF ABUNDANCE

Perhaps the most striking feature of California is the great abundance of wild foods. Acorns provided the dietary staple for most Indian societies. These nuts were gathered in huge quantities as soon as they began falling from trees in the fall. If acorns weren't to your taste, there was a great variety of other wild plants. Roots, bulbs, and tubers were eaten uncooked or roasted in hot ashes. Berries were eaten as they were picked. The Pomo of central California ate plants such as spring clover, and ground the seeds of grasses and small flowering herbs into a dry meal, or made them into small cakes. In the north, the Hupa were fond of the bulbs of lily plants, which had to be steamed in a rock-lined pit for several days before they were ready to eat.

Wicker flails like this Pomo example were used by California Indian women to knock acorns and other seeds out of trees and bushes.

Acorns contain a bitter chemical known as tannin, and they are inedible unless it is removed. The California Indians had a complex method for getting rid of the tannin: Women shelled the acorns, split and dried them, then stored them in large granary baskets. Later, they pounded them into a fine flour with a stone pestle, then leached them with hot water, removing the tannin. Finally, the acorn meal was cooked into a loose mush using heated stones.

MORE THAN JUST PLANTS

Despite the abundance of wild plants, California Indians did not adhere to a strict vegetarian diet. Societies living along swift-moving rivers enjoyed salmon as another dietary staple. Tribes living on the coast had access to a wide variety of ocean fish and shellfish. Deer and smaller game added meat to the diet of most tribes. Larger animals were usually hunted with bows and arrows, while birds and smaller animals were often taken with snares or traps.

The Maidu of California's Central Valley wore elaborate feather decorations for their ceremonial dances, including this crown known as an *unnu'ni*, made from crane feathers.

During the spring salmon run, Hupa men built platforms over pools and used nets with long handles to scoop up the fish. The tribe could usually catch enough in a few weeks to last through the year.

EXTREME CEREMONIES

In California, religious ceremonies varied considerably from tribe to tribe. The Hupa had an almost endless array of taboos to avoid, and engaged in several seasonal rituals. Each of these lasted 10 days and was designed to renew the world for another year. The Luseño tribe put boys through elaborate initiation rites, involving sandpaintings and the painful "ordeal by ants," in which biting ants were sprinkled on the body of the boy being initiated. The Pomo Indians had a unique Ghost Dance that involved eating fire.

This traditional Yurok sweathouse, located at Patrick's Point State Park, is partially underground, with a roof made out of broad redwood planks.

A Tasty Treat?

Some California tribes ate food that most of us would probably find unappetizing. The Pomo, for example, liked to feast on caterpillars known as armyworms. After capturing them by the hundreds in shallow trenches, the Indians would roast the armyworms in hot ashes or boil them for a treat. Angleworms, yellow jacket grubs, and other insects were also enjoyed.

DON'T SWEAT IT

The ease of obtaining food allowed many California Indians to have considerable leisure time. Some tribes in the north built wooden structures known as sweathouses on the banks of rivers. Fire was used to keep the interior extremely hot, much like a modern sauna. After a stay in the sweathouse, people would often plunge into the cold water of the river. The structure was also used as a workshop, clubhouse, and a place for men and boys to sleep.

THE PACIFIC NORTHWEST

The Pacific Northwest is a narrow strip of land and islands on the west coast, cut off from the rest of the continent by snow-capped mountains. More than 50 Indian societies made their homes here, including the Haida, Tlingit, and Kwakwaka'wakw. These tribes developed complex cultures and often possessed huge surpluses of food, even though they had no knowledge of farming. In the midst of such abundance, they put great value on family wealth and status, providing a striking contrast to the more community-centered cultures of other Indian tribes.

Climate: temperate rain forest

Pre-contact population: 210,000

Foods: salmon, halibut, seals, whales

Eyak

Tlingit

Tongass

Nisga'a
Tsimshian
Gitxsan

Haida

Haisla

Nuxalk

Heiltsuk

Kwakwaka'wakw

Nuu-chah-nulth

Comox

Sechelt

Cowichan Musqueam

Makah
Quileute   Skagit
Quinault   Klallam
           Skokomish
Chehalis   Chemakum
              Duwamish
Chinook   Snoqualmie
              Puyallup
Kwalhioqua
Clatskanie   Cowlitz
Tillamook
Siletz
Kalapuya
Alsea
Siuslaw

Coos
     Umpqua
     Takelma
Tututni   Chastacosta

Olympic National Park's Rialto Beach provides a dramatic illustration of the Pacific Northwest environment, with evergreen forests extending all the way to the ocean. The towering land formations known as sea stacks are created by the eroding force of seawater over periods of thousands of years.

A WET AND WOODED ENVIRONMENT

The home of the Northwest Indians stretches more than 2,000 miles (3,218 km) from the panhandle of present-day Alaska south to northern California. At its widest point, the region is only about 150 miles (241 km) across. The rugged mountains drop away abruptly to a maze of inlets, bays, and islands. The climate is surprisingly mild, shaped by the warm Japanese Current, which flows north along the coast, and pushes warm, moisture-laden air in from the sea. The mountains stop most of the clouds from moving farther east, giving the region an annual rainfall of 100 inches (254 cm) or more along the coast. The rain, in turn, creates towering evergreen forests of fir, cedar, spruce, and redwood trees. In addition, spring runoff from the mountains sends rivers cascading down the western slopes to the sea.

Totem poles were often placed at the entrances to houses, rising 40–60 feet (12–18 m) high. The carved blocks usually displayed episodes in a a family's history. The bottom block often contained the front door.

THE USES OF WOOD

All the Indians of the Pacific Northwest made extensive use of wood, especially cedar, and developed extraordinary skills in woodworking. Using a few simple tools and no metal, they felled towering trees and split the logs into boards and beams. Without pegs or nails, they built elaborate plank houses, often large enough for 10 or 12 families. They also used wood for canoes, totem poles, and for an almost endless variety of boxes.

PACIFIC SALMON

FRUIT OF THE SEA

The Northwest tribes relied on the sea for most of their food. As on the Plateau, salmon was the staple. During a salmon run, when the fish swam from inland streams to the ocean, the men used nets, spears, and even their bare hands to catch thousands. Many tribes also caught herring, smelt, and halibut—a deep-water fish that could weigh more than 200 pounds (91 kg). There was also an endless supply of shellfish.

Makah whalers attach floats to a freshly killed whale in Neah Bay, Washington, preparing to drag it to shore with their canoe.

WHALERS OF THE NORTHWEST

Some tribes, such as the Makah, were expert whalers. A whaling party usually consisted of two canoes, carrying eight men each. The harpoons were attached to coils of rope. When a whale was struck, airtight sealskin floats attached to the rope kept the animal from diving too deep. After the whale was dead, the floats were attached to its sides and the canoes towed it to land. The whale provided fresh meat, oil for cooking, and pieces of blubber to chew on.

A ceremonial hat was worn by the host of a potlatch. This Tlingit example is made of spruce roots and topped with an ermine pelt. The painting at the bottom depicts a family crest.

THE POTLACH

A potlatch was a remarkable ceremony, unique to the Northwest region, in which a chief or wealthy man distributed great amounts of wealth and gifts to his guests, emphasizing his status in the tribe. Sometimes the event took several years to prepare. Family, friends, and supporters prepared food, made carved boxes or figures, wove piles of blankets, and collected deerskins and otter furs. The potlatch ceremony lasted several days, with feasting, dancing, and games. Canoes loaded with food challenged the guests to eat constantly. On the last day of the potlatch, the host gave guests departing gifts as they left, with the most elaborate gifts going to the most important guests.

The Prized Candlefish

One of the favorite fishes of the Northwest tribes was the *eulachon*, or "candlefish." This small fish holds so much oil that a string pressed into it as a wick will burn for days. To obtain the fish, the northern tribes—Tlingit, Haida, and Tsimshian—had to trade with the Nisga'a, who controlled the rivers where it was most common.

The Haida were one of the largest tribes in the Northwest, numbering nearly 10,000 at the time of European contact. Their villages were located on the Queen Charlotte Islands off the coast of British Columbia, with smaller numbers on the southern part of Prince of Wales Island. Although they were geographically isolated, the Haida developed an elaborate culture, and were known for being outstanding artists with wood.

A Haida man stands before a traditional cedar-plank house, complete with totem pole, in this photograph from 1884.

EASY PREPARATION

During the summer, meal preparation was easy for the Haida. They had various ways of preparing and curing salmon, some of which involved dipping the fish into candlefish oil. Berries were eaten as they were picked. Foods were often baked in outdoor pits on hot stones, then covered with seaweed for moisture. In the house, meals could be boiled in watertight boxes or baskets by dropping hot stones into the water. In addition, Haida women pounded dried roots and fruit into a dough that was formed into cakes.

This Haida club was used to stun halibut.

SEASONAL RHYTHMS

The life of the Haida changed with the seasons. During the summer months, they worked hard catching and preparing salmon. The whole family took part and enjoyed the work. To catch the salmon, the men and older boys usually stretched a large net, or weir, across a river to trap the salmon on their return to the sea. As the men emptied baskets of fish onto the grassy bank, the women and girls gathered and cleaned them. They put most of the salmon on racks. Some were sun-dried, others were smoked under low fires. The preserved salmon would last until the following year. In the winter, the Haida moved from streamside shelters to their permanent cedar-plank houses. During the cooler months, they spent most of their time making clothing or working on carvings and other woodworking projects.

The remains of totem poles line the shore at Skungwa'ai, a former Haida village located on Anthony Island in the Gwaii Haanas National Park.

MASTERS OF WOODWORKING

In a region known for skilled woodworkers, the Haida were among the very best. Building a house was the most demanding and time-consuming of their woodworking projects. Like other tribes, the Haida had no metal tools, and the task was often spread over several years. The Haida also displayed extraordinary skill at making canoes. These boats ranged in size from small dugouts designed for two men to large war canoes, measuring up to 70 feet (21 m) in length. The Haida also made totem poles, as well as boxes in many sizes with elaborately carved lids.

This carving is a model of a Haida grave house. In a real grave house the coffin would have been inserted through the hole at the base, and the carvings on the pole would relate to the deceased.

This Haida pole was used to mark the grave of an important member of the tribe. The bottom carving depicts a bird of prey.

THE CYCLE OF LIFE

Among the Haida, every phase of a person's life was accompanied by special ceremonies. Young children spent much of their time with their grandparents, who instructed them in the tribe's stories and songs. Around age six, they began following their parents and learning adult skills. At about age 13, boys were sent on a vision quest, living alone in the wilderness for at least five days. Girls were ready for marriage at 14, boys at 15. A wedding was the occasion for a great party lasting several days. In old age, the Haida were treated with great respect. When someone died, the body was placed in a box and tied high in a tree in the village cemetery, or placed in a special grave house. His name was never mentioned again, out of fear he might hear it and try to return.

Shamans were very important in Haida culture, and helped perform the rituals that gave structure to people's lives.

CEDAR-BARK CLOTHING

Although much of their clothing was made from deerskin, the Haida and other coastal tribes made some clothing from cedar bark. To make the fabric, women stripped the bark off young trees, then soaked it in saltwater for several days, after which it was pounded until the fibers were easily pulled apart. Finally, the fibers were woven into cloth. The cedar cloth was used to make excellent blankets, in addition to capes and hats that were both water-repellent and warm.

Cedar cloth was used by many coastal tribes. Here, a Kwakwaka'wakw woman prepares the bark, wearing a finished cape.

To see how the Haida lived after contact with Europeans, see pp.110–111.

TOTEM POLES

Totem poles served many purposes for the people of the Pacific Northwest. Some represented a family's history and status, while others depicted familiar legends. The poles shown here, located in Stanley Park in Vancouver, Canada, give an idea of the variety of forms and function that these traditional artworks can possess.

Chief Wakas Pole is a replica of a pole that stood at the entrance to the house of a Northwest chief.

Oscar Maltipi Pole depicts a mythical being known as Thunderbird at the top.

Beaver Crest Pole tells the story of how the Tait family of the Nisga'a tribe adopted the beaver as their crest.

Kakaso'las Pole was made in 1955 by Ellen Neel, the first female carver in the Northwest.

Ga'akstalas Pole depicts figures from Kwakwaka'wakw myths, such as Red Cedar-bark Man, who gave people the first canoe.

Sky Chief Pole depicts many figures from Nuu-chah-nulth mythology. At the top, Sky Chief is holding the moon.

Thunderbird House Post is a replica of a carved post that held up the ceiling of a house.

THE NORTHEAST WOODLANDS

The Northeast was a complex geographic region consisting of mountain ranges, lakes, rivers, valleys, flatlands, hills, and coast. Throughout the region, the dominant element was the forest. Thick blocks of towering trees formed an almost solid canopy over the entire Northeast. More than 50 Indian nations were living in the region when the first Europeans arrived, with a total population estimated at 500,000. The ancestors of many tribes had been living there for more than 11,000 years.

Climate: temperate forest

Pre-contact population: 503,200

Foods: corn, beans, squash, wild rice, deer

Micmac
Malecite
Passamaquoddy
Penobscot
Abnaki
Ojibwe
Algonkin
Nipissing
Pennacook
Menominee
Huron
Nipmuc
Pequot
Massachuset
Tobacco
Neutral
Mohawk
Mohegan
Mahican
Wampanoag
Narraganset
Ottawa
Oneida
Winnebago
Potawatomi
Erie
Onondaga
Cayuga
Seneca
Wappinger
Montauk
Sauk
Fox
Delaware
Kickapoo
Miami
Susquehannock
Peoria
Wea
Nanticoke
Kaskaskia
Piankashaw
Illinois
Powhatan
Shawnee
Nottaway
Meherrin
Tuscarora
Weapemeoc
Secotan
Pamlico

The corn harvest was an important time for Northeast tribes. Although this illustration shows a man helping with the harvest, this would have been unusual. Women were responsible for farming, assisted by children and occasionally elderly men.

DIVISION OF LABOR

All the Northeast Indian nations hunted, fished, and gathered wild foods. Most, however, were also farmers, and it was this dependable food supply that enabled them to live in settled villages. Women tended the crops, always centered on the "three sisters"—corn, beans, and squash, and they were also specialists in gathering wild plants. Aided by the children, women filled baskets or deerskin sacks with berries, grapes, nuts, and a wide variety of roots, herbs, and leafy plants. Meanwhile, the men engaged in hunting and fishing, with deer being the primary game. In the west of the region, food sources varied slightly. Most of the western tribes hunted bison in addition to deer, and some relied on wild rice rather than corn. Together, the men, women, and children provided a rich and varied diet for the tribe.

BOUNTY OF THE WOODS

Northeast tribes relied on the forest for all the raw materials of life. For transportation, they used canoes, made by sewing pieces of birchbark over a cedar frame, using tough pieces of bark or root. Baskets were crafted using willow splints, reeds, sweet grasses, or bark. Smaller baskets were often made of porcupine quills.

Indian canoes were triumphs of engineering. The natural grain of the bark sheets can be seen in this model of a Malecite vessel.

A NATURAL WARDROBE

Throughout the Northeast woodlands, most clothing was made of deerskin, the pieces sewn together with rawhide. Men usually wore a breechcloth over a belt, often with fringed leggings. Women wore a sleeveless dress or a skirt, and often wore leggings as well. Feathers and bits of fur were used for decoration. Men, women, and children wore moccasins, often lined with rabbit fur in winter.

This **Penobscot jacket** shows European influence in its shape and glass-bead embroidery, but is still made from deerskin, a traditional material used by most Northeast tribes.

Endless Forest

1704 Although the forest was home for the Northeast Indians, many European colonists found it frightening. In 1704 Sarah Kemble Knight traveled alone from Boston to New York and wrote the following account.

My guide suddenly moved rapidly out of sight, leaving me in the darkness of the forest. There was only a glimmering from the spangled sky, which only served to make every object more formidable and frightening. Each lifeless Trunk, with its shattered limbs, appeared like an Armed Enemy . . . I was never so eager to be under clear sky again. Is the whole land plagued with such forests?

False Face masks, such as this Cayuga example, were carved into a living tree, then removed.

MASKS AND MEDICINE

Like other Indian societies, Northeast Indian nations believed in a variety of nature spirits, and relied heavily on shamans. Among the Iroquois tribes, ailments involving the head, shoulders, or limbs were healed by members of the False Face Society, known for their striking wooden masks. Their ceremonies were held in the communal longhouse at the patient's request. Cured patients were required to join the society themselves. In the spring and fall, members of the society visited and purified every household in the tribe.

The Importance of Tobacco

In most Northeast nations, men grew small plots of tobacco, even though women normally tended the crops. The plant was smoked in a long pipe called a calumet, and was thought to be helpful in communicating with spirits. Tobacco was also smoked at tribal meetings, where the pipe was always handed around the circle of men in a clockwise direction. At the time, the Indians were not aware of the health risks associated with smoking.

THE IROQUOIS

The Iroquois Confederacy was composed of five Indian nations: the Seneca, Cayuga, Onondaga, Oneida, and Mohawk. Altough these tribes once fought with each other, they later banded together under an agreement known as the Great Law of Peace, which used a system of checks and balances to ensure fairness and stability. Many think this government served as a model for the Constitution of the United States. Unlike the Constitution, however, the Iroquois agreement gave women real political power within the society.

When Was It Formed?

In the 19th century, American poet Henry Wadsworth Longfellow wrote a poem about the Iroquois, leading many to believe that the confederacy was formed in the 1700s. However, experts now think that the Great Law of Peace was established much earlier, probably in the 1300s or 1400s—making it one of the world's earliest democratic governments.

THE PEOPLE OF THE LONGHOUSE

The Iroquois called themselves "the people of the longhouse," due to the dwellings in which they lived. Iroquois longhouses consisted of a frame of poles and beams, with those supporting the roof bent to form arches. The walls and roofs were made from tiles of bark. Each longhouse was large enough for 10 or more families, with pairs of families sharing a cooking fire in the center. Shelves along the walls were used for sleeping and storage. There was a door at either end, but no windows. Smoke escaped through roof holes, but the dwellings were generally dark and smoky. A village was made up of several longhouses, inhabited by related families, surrounded by a stockade of upright poles. Some neighboring tribes also lived in longhouses, but their designs often differed from those of the Iroquois. For example, Algonquian longhouses tended to be lower and more rounded, causing them to resemble extended wigwams (see p.65).

An Iroquois village was made up of multiple longhouses, belonging to related families. This 17th-century engraving, which depicts a French attack on an Onondaga village, is considered one of the earliest reliable illustrations of an Iroquois settlement.

A longhouse was a home for multiple Iroquois families, and could be up to 150 feet (45 m) long. This model represents an eight-family house.

DAILY LIFE

In Iroquois society, everyone was expected to show respect for both children and the elderly. Children learned from their parents and grandparents, and they also developed skills through games. Meals were informal, and people generally ate when they were hungry. A stew consisting of deer meat and a variety of root vegetables was kept warm by the fire, and each person filled his or her own bowl. Occasionally, several families ate together. Ceremonies and festivals were held throughout the year. These included the Green Corn Harvest, celebrating the first harvest of corn, and the Midwinter Renewal Festival.

Husk faces were worn during the Midwinter Festival to ensure a good harvest.

Women had real power in Iroquois society, a feature that has often been admired by later advocates of women's rights.

THE ROLE OF WOMEN

One unique feature of the Iroquois Confederacy was the prominent role it gave to women. Each Iroquois clan, made up of several related families, was headed by a woman known as a clan mother. The clan mothers, in turn, chose 50 men as *sachems*, who then formed a governing council representing all of the Five Nations. The council could decide matters of war and peace, but not the internal matters of any nation. If one of the sachems failed to act in accordance with Iroquois philosophy, the clan mother who appointed him would talk to him about the problem. If necessary, she could have him replaced.

HIAWATHA AND DEGANAWIDAH

According to the oral history of the Iroquois, the five nations used to fight constantly. One Iroquois named Hiawatha made several attempts at peace, but was unsuccessful until he met a Huron prophet named Deganawidah, who shared the same goals. With Hiawatha's speaking skills and Deganawidah's vision, the two were a persuasive force. The result was the Great Law of Peace, which created the Iroquois Confederacy. By tradition, the Great Council of the confederacy met around a fire that was tended by the Onondaga.

The Sixth Nation

Long after contact with Europeans, the Tuscarora tribe, originally from North Carolina, asked for admission to the Iroquois Confederacy as a sixth nation. The Iroquois Council accepted them, although not as an equal member.

Hiawatha worked to create peace among the Iroquois, in cooperation with Deganawidah. In 1855, Henry Wadsworth Longfellow wrote a popular poem called *The Song of Hiawatha*, but it has little in common with the traditional Iroquois tale.

The Ojibwe were one of the largest Woodland nations. They lived in a heavily forested region west of Lake Superior and in large areas of southern Canada. According to their oral histories, they once lived near a great sea that tasted of salt—probably the Atlantic Ocean. Experts believe they moved to their inland home sometime during the 15th or 16th century.

SURVIVING IN THE FORESTS

The Ojibwe homeland was filled with forests, as well as countless lakes, rivers, streams, and ponds. The people made clearings next to water, and many of the clans moved to more sheltered areas for the bitterly cold winters. During the summer, men cleared garden plots and women planted the basic "three sisters" crops—corn, beans, and squash. Most villages relied more heavily on hunting, fishing, and gathering wild foods than on farming. This did not always provide a stable food supply, so winter hunger and even starvation were a danger. To avoid such disasters every village tried to store as much preserved food as possible.

The Ojibwe often lived next to their region's many lakes and rivers. In this engraving, a group of Ojibwe use bark to repair a broken canoe.

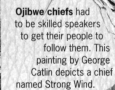

Ojibwe chiefs had to be skilled speakers to get their people to follow them. This painting by George Catlin depicts a chief named Strong Wind.

CLANS AND BANDS

Several related families formed a clan, named after a bird or animal—Ojibwe clans included Crane, Catfish, Bear, Loon, and Marten. Several clans formed a band, usually containing 300 to 400 people. Several bands, in turn, made up a tribe. Tribes were relatively informal and the chief of a tribe had to persuade his people to follow him. This made oratory—the ability to speak in public—the most important skill for an Ojibwe chief.

THE WONDER OF WAMPUM

Wampum belts were popular among the Ojibwe and other Northeast tribes. To make wampum, the Indians cut white-and-purple quahog clamshells into small beads. The beads were then polished, strung together, and woven into belts of 10 to 20 strands. Wampum belts could be used as money, jewelry, or even as documents. When the beads were placed in patterns, they could record a message, such as an agreement between groups, or even a long tribal history. Today wampum belts are prized items in museums.

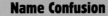

Wampum belts were woven from beads made of shells. The belts could be many feet long, and the purple beads were considered twice as valuable as the white ones.

This decorative pouch displays many key elements of Ojibwe design. The tassels at the bottom are formed from dyed porcupine quills and deer fur. The winged figures represent mythical flying beings known as thunderers.

Wigwams could be made from whatever materials were available. This example, flanked by European-style tents, blends traditional materials with more modern fabrics.

BUILDING A WIGWAM

Ojibwe houses, called wigwams, looked like large, upside-down bowls. To make a wigwam, the Indians started with a frame of poles, which they bent into a dome shape. These frames were then covered with large pieces of overlapping birchbark, along with woven mats or deerskins, depending on what was available. The pieces were tied together with strips of rawhide.

A DECORATIVE TOUCH

Like other Northeast tribes, the Ojibwe made most of their clothing out of deerskin and used decoration to emphasize their tribal identity. The Ojibwe garments were known for their attractive fringes, which were often 12 inches (30 cm) long or more. The tribe also made creative use of dyed porcupine quills, which they added to many everyday items. Wampum beads were popular decorations, as was face and body paint.

Wild Rice

Wild rice grew in shallow lakes and was a special crop of the Woodland Indians. Two people, often husband and wife, harvested the rice from a canoe. While the person in front paddled, the one in the back bent clumps of the ripened heads and beat them with a stick so the rice fell into the boat.

Algonquian villages often included a longhouse, where the chief and his family lived, as well as smaller wigwams. Most houses had inner and outer frameworks made from saplings and walls made from pieces of bark. This replicated village stands at the site of the Institute for American Indian Studies in Connecticut.

Before 1500, an estimated 286,000 Native people lived along the rivers of the Southeast. Large societies such as the Cherokee were usually divided into small villages. Most groups lived by farming supplemented by hunting, fishing, and gathering. A mild, moist climate allowed them to get by with relatively simple clothing and shelter.

Saponi
Monacan
Tutelo
Eno
Yuchi
Koasati   Sugeree   Woccon
           Cheraw Catawba
Cherokee   Wateree Waccamaw
                            Pedee
Chickasaw
              Tuskegee   Cusabo
Tunica
     Ofo   Napochi   Creek
Caddo   Chakchiuma   Hitchiti
                 Alabama
                      Chiaha Yamasee
                      Tamathli Guale
        Yazoo   Tohome
   Taensa Choctaw   Chacato
Hasinai Natchez
        Houma   Mobila Apalachee
Bidai   Biloxi Pensacola
   Atakapa Chitimacha
            Chawasha
                                Timucua
                                  Ais
                            Seminole
                            Calusa
                               Tekesta

Climate: temperate forest, wetland

Pre-contact population: 286,000

Foods: corn, beans, squash, deer, turkey

The Natchez

The Natchez were notable for retaining the customs of the ancient mound-building cultures (see pp.30–31) after they had died out elsewhere. Like the Mississippians, they believed their chief was descended from the sun god. In the 1700s, the Natchez were destroyed in a series of conflicts with the French.

GEOGRAPHY AND SETTLEMENT PATTERNS

The diverse geography of the Southeast region influenced settlement patterns. Along the Atlantic coast, a broad, level plain was crossed by rivers flowing from the mountains east into the sea. This area is known as the Tidewater, because the ocean saltwater moves upstream with the tide. Many Native societies lived in small villages along the riverbanks. Farther inland, in the hills and mountains of the Blue Ridge and Great Smoky Mountains, the Cherokee were one of the largest nations. They lived in parts of seven present-day states, with the largest numbers in Tennessee, Alabama, and Georgia. The hills and mountains in this area provided protection from other tribes. Protection was also afforded by the Cherokee's sizable villages of about 50 families, surrounded by sturdy stockades. A very different way of life was followed by tribes in the low-lying areas of marsh and swamp. The Calusa Indians of Florida lived in thatched houses called *chickees*, built on platforms above the water level. They traveled and went fishing in dugout canoes.

Dugout canoes were used by Florida Indians for a variety of purposes. Here, they are depicted bringing crops to a communal storehouse. This image is based on an original by artist Jacques Le Moyne, who joined a French expedition to America in the 1560s.

Lacrosse players often wore elaborate game outfits, as shown in this George Catlin painting. On the left is Thirsts-for-Stone, a champion Choctaw player.

LITTLE BROTHER OF WAR

Lacrosse was played in many regions of North America, but it was played with particular enthusiasm in the Southeast. Known as the "little brother of war," the game was originally much more violent than the version we know today. Teams sometimes had more than 100 members each, serious injuries were common, and players were sometimes killed during a match. Each player held two sticks with webbing at the end. These sticks were used to pass a ball made of wood or deerskin from person to person, with the ultimate goal being to send it flying through the goalposts of the opposing team. Spectators often bet heavily on the matches.

A HOUSE FOR ALL SEASONS

Among the Creek, all towns were designated as either "white towns," where ceremonies devoted to peace were held, or "red towns," which were geared toward war. Within the towns, dwellings were organized into cool summer houses and warm winter lodges. The summer houses often consisted of nothing more than a platform on stilts, with a thatched roof. In good weather, the Council of Elders met in an outdoor square. In bad weather, they met in a round house up to 25 feet (7.5 m) high.

The Yuchi of Tennessee used feather fans like this one during the sacred dances of the Green Corn Ceremony. The white feathers mirrored the white clothing worn by the dancers, as well as their audience.

THE ANNUAL BUSK

One of the most important rituals in the Southeast was the Green Corn Ceremony, also known as the Busk. It was held when the corn ripened, and served as a way to give thanks for the harvest and mark the beginning of a new year. At the start of the ceremony, members of the tribe would engage in ritual purification, which could involve bathing in a stream or river, or drinking an herbal concoction that induced vomiting. A series of dances was then performed around a sacred fire, and a feast was held, in which the year's corn harvest was tasted for the first time. Typically, minor crimes and debts were forgiven during the Busk.

A Creek council house was a round, windowless building with a roof made from tree trunks. During a meeting, the elders would sit around a central fire.

THE CHEROKEE

The Cherokee lived in the foothills and mountains of the Blue Ridge and Great Smoky ranges. With a population of about 22,000, the Cherokee made up the largest Indian nation in the Southeast. Their villages covered a large area that extended over what would become parts of eight states. The most densely populated areas were in Georgia, North Carolina, and Tennessee.

A RICH AND VARIED NATURAL MENU

By combining hunting, fishing, gathering wild foods, and farming, the Cherokee enjoyed a varied and nutritious diet. Their favorite foods included corn soup, bean dumplings, and hominy (corn that was bleached white). Other favorite dishes were based on wild foods they gathered or on animals they hunted. Bread and pudding were made from chestnuts, and roast turkey was a popular meal. Men and boys enjoyed hunting on the forested slopes of the Blue Ridge and Great Smoky Mountains. The big game included deer, elk, bear, and occasionally bison from small herds that had roamed east from the Great Plains. In addition to turkeys, the Cherokee hunted migratory birds such as Canada geese.

Cherokee clothing consisted of softened deerskin in styles similar to those of other woodland peoples. Their winter clothing was somewhat more distinctive, because the winters in the highlands tended to be cold and snowy. During these colder months, the Cherokee wore long fur-lined robes, and the women's were decorated with turkey feathers.

Cherokee summer houses were rectangular, with thatched roofs and walls coated with earth or clay. In the winter, the Cherokee moved to small, round homes that provided more protection from the cold.

TENNESSEE

Tanasi was the name of a major Cherokee town. It later lent its name to the state of Tennessee.

The Great Smoky Mountains are named for the natural haze that forms over their peaks. They were once prime hunting grounds for the Cherokee.

PEACE CHIEFS AND WAR CHIEFS

As was the case in many Indian societies, Cherokee families were members of clans. In the Cherokee's case, the clans were headed by women. Each of the seven clans—Bear, Bird, Blue, Deer, Long Hair, Potato, and Wolf—had several hundred families. A town was home to about 50 families and was surrounded by a stockade. Each town had two chiefs: the peace chief, who wore a white headdress, was in power when the Cherokee were at peace. In wartime, a war chief with a red headdress took over. The two chiefs were also members of the town council, along with seven elders representing the clans. The town council worked with a Council of Beloved Women, one from each clan, to resolve town problems and improve conditions. The council house was located in the center of town and was traditionally seven-sided. Many of the town's ceremonies were held in, or in front of, the council building.

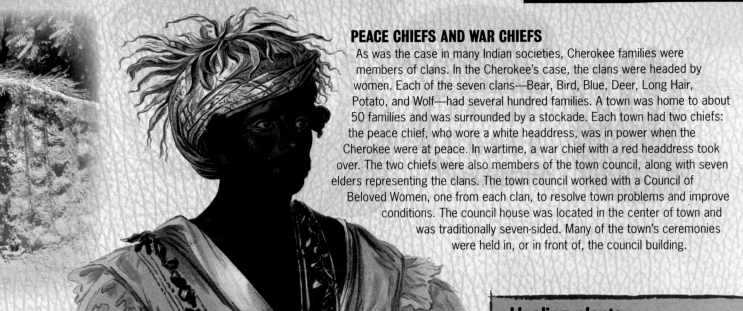

Cherokee chiefs were traditionally divided into peace chiefs who wore white headdresses, like the one shown in this portrait, and war chiefs who wore red headdresses.

This ceremonial wand was used in the Eagle Dance, which was used to celebrate both peace and war. The wand is decorated with eagle feathers.

Healing plants

The Cherokee were famous for their skill in locating herbs and other plants that were useful in healing specific illnesses. Spirea, for example, was found to help with headaches and other pains. (It was later used in the formula for aspirin.)

SPIREA

A YEAR OF CEREMONIES

Religious ceremonies were spread throughout the year. As much as the event itself, the Cherokee people enjoyed the weeks of preparation, which involved making masks, drums, costumes, and headdresses. Every festival included music and dances. As in other Southeast societies, the Green Corn Ceremony was a major event, representing a fresh start to the year. The Booger Ceremony, on the other hand, was held strictly for fun. In this ceremony, masked dancers made their way around the village, making fun of the Cherokee's enemies. Ceremonies were also held to mark important milestones in people's lives. When a couple decided to marry, celebrations were held in front of the town council house. The bride and groom arrived covered by blue blankets. A priest or priestess blessed the couple and, as songs were sung, removed the blue blankets and replaced them with a single white one. The birth of a child was another occasion for celebrating. In one ceremony, the infant was taken to a river, where a prayer was said for a long and healthy life. This was followed by a naming ceremony, in which a respected older woman gave the child a permanent name.

THE ARCTIC AND SUBARCTIC

The Arctic and Subarctic are adjoining geographic regions that cover the northern third of North America. The Arctic stretches from the Aleutian Islands across the northern edge of the continent to Greenland, a distance of about 5,000 miles (1600 km). Just below that coastal belt is the Subarctic, which covers a large area of today's northern Canada. Both regions can be extremely cold, making survival a daunting challenge. From the Cree in the south to the Inuit in the north, Native people have shown remarkable ingenuity in adapting to these inhospitable lands.

Climate: tundra, taiga
Pre-contact population: 246,200
Foods: seals, whales, caribou, salmon

Siberian Yupik
Siberian Yupik
Inupiat
Koyukon
Central Yupik
Ingalik
Tanana
Mackenzie Inuit
Aleut
Tanaina
Kutchin
Hare
Saschutkenne
Aleut
Han
Mountain
Nabesna
Ahtena
Pacific Gulf Yupik
Tutchone
Tagish
Dogrib
Yellowknife
Copper Inuit
Caribou Inuit
Tahltan
Kaska
Tsetsaut
Slave
Sekani
Chipewyan
Carrier
Beaver
Swampy Cree
Chilcotin
Western Woods Cree
Cree
Northern Ojibwe
Saulteaux
Southern Ojibwe
Algonkin
Polar Inuit
Iglulik Inuit
Netsilik Inuit
Southampton Inuit
East Greenland Inuit
West Greenland Inuit
Baffinland Inuit
Labrador Inuit
Naskapi
Mistassini Cree
Montagnais
Tête de Boule Cree
Beothuk

THE FROZEN NORTH

The Arctic is one of the world's most challenging environments. In January, temperatures often reach –40°F (–40°C). The landscape, known as tundra, is flat, except for the Brooks Range in Alaska. The soil remains frozen all year, except for a few inches that thaw during the brief summer. For those few weeks, the tundra is covered with grasses and colorful wildflowers. All in all, the Arctic is a severe test of humans' ability to adapt.

Alexandra Fjord, on Ellesmere Island in northern Canada, demonstrates the stark beauty of the Arctic region.

CHANGING NAMES

For many years, the word *Eskimo* was used to refer to the Native people of the Arctic. However, this term is now considered insulting by many people, due to a belief that it means "eaters of raw meat." Today, the word *Inuit* has largely replaced *Eskimo* in Greenland and Canada, but the situation is trickier in Alaska, since some Native societies there do not consider themselves to be Inuits. Thus, the term *Eskimo* is still common in the state, along with *Alaska Native*.

SUBARCTIC HUNTERS

Most of the Subarctic is covered by vast areas of forest called the *taiga*. Summers are short and cool, and winters are long and cold, though snowfall is usually light. A number of fairly small Indian societies, including the Beaver, Cree, and Kutchin, are scattered throughout the region. These tribes traveled great distances by canoe and toboggan to follow herds of game such as caribou and elk. Some tribes also fished and and hunted sea mammals, while those located near large rivers became salmon fishers.

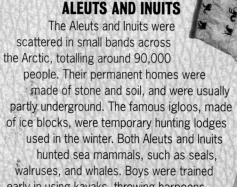

Snowshoes allowed Subarctic people to hunt in areas covered by deep snow.

INUIT SNOW GOGGLES

ALEUTS AND INUITS

The Aleuts and Inuits were scattered in small bands across the Arctic, totalling around 90,000 people. Their permanent homes were made of stone and soil, and were usually partly underground. The famous igloos, made of ice blocks, were temporary hunting lodges used in the winter. Both Aleuts and Inuits hunted sea mammals, such as seals, walruses, and whales. Boys were trained early in using kayaks, throwing harpoons, and handling spears on rough seas, while girls learned to cut, smoke, and preserve the meat of the whale.

All Inuit anoraks protected against the cold. This one, made of seal intestines, protected against water as well.

INUIT ANIMAL AMULET

THE POWER OF AMULETS

Arctic and Subarctic tribes believed strongly in the power of amulets. An amulet could be any small object the owner hoped would bring good luck: an unusual seashell, a piece of driftwood, or an eagle's feather. Carved animal amulets were thought to bring success at hunting the animal depicted. Amulets were placed on clothing, tools, tents, and kayaks, and the loss of an amulet was considered a great disaster.

To make an igloo, Inuits first built a circular base of ice blocks, and then gradually added more rows.

Comb morion helmets were often worn by the Spanish conquistadors who explored the Southwest.

CHAPTER 3

FIRST ENCOUNTERS WITH EUROPEANS

The New World meets the Old World

In 1492, Christopher Columbus arrived at an island in the West Indies, off the coast of Florida. Although he never set foot on the North American mainland, his voyage unleashed a flood of Europeans who came to explore and colonize the continent. America's Native people first encountered these Europeans at different times in different places—from the 1500s in Florida to the 1800s in some areas of the Plains. Depending on the circumstances, these meetings took many different forms. Sometimes, they were occasions for wonder and excitement. Other times, they led immediately to bloodshed and fear.

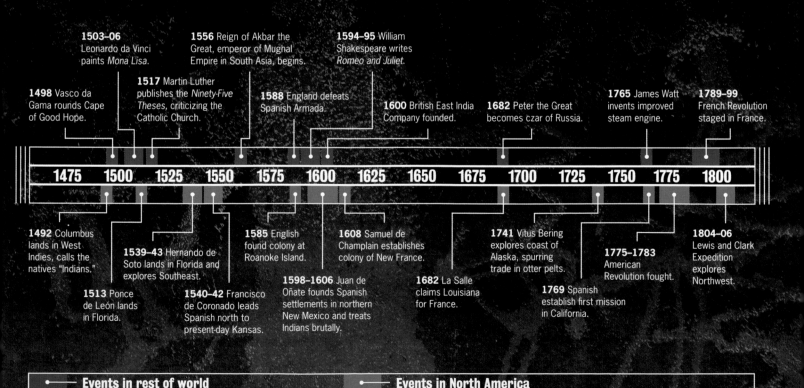

1503–06 Leonardo da Vinci paints *Mona Lisa*.

1556 Reign of Akbar the Great, emperor of Mughal Empire in South Asia, begins.

1594–95 William Shakespeare writes *Romeo and Juliet*.

1517 Martin Luther publishes the *Ninety-Five Theses*, criticizing the Catholic Church.

1498 Vasco da Gama rounds Cape of Good Hope.

1588 England defeats Spanish Armada.

1600 British East India Company founded.

1682 Peter the Great becomes czar of Russia.

1765 James Watt invents improved steam engine.

1789–99 French Revolution staged in France.

| 1475 | 1500 | 1525 | 1550 | 1575 | 1600 | 1625 | 1650 | 1675 | 1700 | 1725 | 1750 | 1775 | 1800 |

1492 Columbus lands in West Indies, calls the natives "Indians."

1539–43 Hernando de Soto lands in Florida and explores Southeast.

1585 English found colony at Roanoke Island.

1608 Samuel de Champlain establishes colony of New France.

1741 Vitus Bering explores coast of Alaska, spurring trade in otter pelts.

1804–06 Lewis and Clark Expedition explores Northwest.

1513 Ponce de León lands in Florida.

1540–42 Francisco de Coronado leads Spanish north to present-day Kansas.

1598–1606 Juan de Oñate founds Spanish settlements in northern New Mexico and treats Indians brutally.

1682 La Salle claims Louisiana for France.

1775–1783 American Revolution fought.

1769 Spanish establish first mission in California.

● Events in rest of world   ● Events in North America

EUROPEANS EXPLORE THE SOUTHEAST

Some of the earliest European explorations of the North American mainland took place in the Southeast, the area closest to the islands visited by Columbus. Many of these early explorers were attempting to establish colonies, while others were simply looking for gold. However, the newcomers often found the task of establishing a foothold in the New World to be more difficult than they'd hoped.

THE SPANISH IN FLORIDA

In 1513, over 20 years after the first voyage of Columbus, a Spanish conquistador named Juan Ponce de León led a small force into the North American mainland, naming the area *Florida* after the Spanish word for "flowery." Like many European explorers, he came in search of gold; when that failed, he decided to take slaves. However, the Calusa Indians had no intention of allowing any of their people to be forced into slavery. The Calusa had built a strong empire, relying heavily on the sea. They lined up 80 war canoes to block the advance of the Spanish. After two days of fighting, the Spanish retreated. This was the first incident of violence between Europeans and Indians on the soil of the future United States.

In 1521, Ponce de León returned, planning to build a settlement. The Calusa again resisted, and this time Ponce de León was struck in the leg by a poisoned arrow. He retreated with his forces to Cuba. Within a few days, all those wounded by the poisoned arrows died, including Ponce de León himself.

More than four decades passed before the Spanish were able to establish a settlement at St. Augustine in 1565. This was the earliest permanent European settlement in the future United States. The relations between the settlers at St. Augustine and the Timucua Indians were generally peaceful, and many Indians were converted to Christianity.

DE SOTO'S VIOLENT EXPLORATIONS

In 1539, Spanish conquistador Hernando de Soto landed on Florida's west coast with 550 soldiers, work gangs, horses, attack dogs, and pigs. Over the years, various exaggerated accounts had given rise to the belief that there were seven fabulous golden cities located in the area, known as the Seven Cities of Cíbola. De Soto headed inland, hoping to find these cities, and to bring back some of the fabulous treasure they contained.

Wherever the Spanish army went, de Soto showed ruthless determination. Like many Europeans, he saw non-Christians as inherently inferior to Christians, and he treated the Indians accordingly. In addition, the Spanish had already conquered the Aztec and Inca Empires by this time, and built the

Hernando de Soto reached the Mississippi River with his army in 1541.

Roanoke Island is shown in the upper left of this map, which depicts the English colonists arriving in North America in 1584.

empire of New Spain upon the ruins (see p.27). For de Soto, this set a precdent for the destruction of Native societies to the north.

For three years, de Soto led his army through the Southeast, encountering Creeks, Chickasaws, Cherokees, Mobilas, and several other Indian societies. When a tribe showed signs of resisting, de Soto's men attacked, burning villages and killing thousands. Slaves were placed in chains and neck collars, tribal leaders were tortured and murdered, and anything valuable was stolen.

Furious about the suffering inflicted by the Spanish, the Choctaws made their travels more difficult by stealing Spanish horses. Soon after reaching the Gulf of Mexico in 1542, de Soto became ill and died. The rest of de Soto's men made their way back to Mexico through Texas, leaving behind a trail of anger and fear.

THE ENGLISH ON THE ATLANTIC COAST

In 1584, sea captain Sir Walter Raleigh persuaded ambitious merchants that it would be profitable to establish English colonies on the North American coast. As a result, a small colony was started on Roanoke Island, off the coast of

North Carolina. However, friction developed between the English and the Indians, and the colonists went back home. In 1587, Raleigh sent out a new group of 117 colonists, determined to give it another try.

Shortly afterward, John White, the governor of Roanoke, went back to England for supplies, but his return to the colony was delayed. When he finally got back, the colony was deserted, with no clue to the colonists' fate. All that remained was the word *Croatan*, the name of a local Indian tribe, carved into a tree.

To this day, no one is sure what happened to the Roanoke colonists. Twenty years later, in 1607, the English established the colony of Jamestown, the first permanent English settlement in the New World.

Roanoke's Artistic Governor

John White, governor of the Roanoke Colony, was an excellent artist. His watercolors provide some of our earliest images of North American Indians.

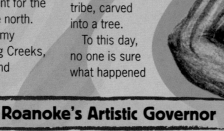

The Indians in the area near Roanoke are considered part of the Northeast culture group. This chief was painted by John White.

FIRST MEETINGS IN THE NORTHEAST

Europeans had many reasons to explore the Northeast of North America. Some hoped to find wealth similar to that of Central and South America. Others hoped to find a Northwest Passage, or water route to Asia. Finally, there was the desire to convert the "savages" to Christianity and add to the territory of one's country.

THE FRENCH APPROACH

By the early 1500s, French sea captains had found rich fishing banks around the mouth of the St. Lawrence River, in modern Quebec. Hoping to find a Northwest Passage, French explorer Jacques Cartier sailed up the St. Lawrence in 1534. Unfortunately, Cartier's trip was cut short by impassable rapids. However, when he returned to the river a few years later, he was interested to note that the Indians would trade excellent beaver pelts for a handful of glass beads or a few inexpensive trinkets.

The trade in beaver fur rapidly became a source of great wealth for France and other European countries, while at the same time revolutionizing the way of life of many Indian societies. The first people of the Northeast would soon gain new forms of wealth, power, and prestige—but competition among tribes would eventually lead to warfare.

Beaver fur was excellent for making hats, creating a huge demand in Europe.

THE AGE OF THE FUR TRADE

The French government followed up Cartier's explorations by sending Samuel de Champlain to the St. Lawrence River in 1608. Over a total of 11 voyages, Champlain established trading posts at Quebec City and Montreal. By 1664, these trading posts were incorporated into the colony of New France.

The French also moved westward. Explorers, traders, missionaries, soldiers, and freelance trappers/traders known as *coureurs de bois* ("runners of the woods") pushed west over rivers and lakes. The *coureurs de bois* often lived among the Indians. Many even married Indian women, and were welcomed as family members by their wives' tribe or nation. This friendly approach helped the French maintain good relations with many tribes, including the Ottawa, Ojibwe, Fox, and above all the Huron, whose villages stretched along what is now the southern border of Canada.

TERRITORIAL EXPANSION

In the 1670s, Louis Joliet, a fur trader, and Father Jacques Marquette, a Jesuit scholar, made a 2,500-mile (4,023 km) canoe journey west to Lake Michigan and Lake Winnebago, then south to the Mississippi River and on to the Gulf of Mexico. They discovered that the Mississippi did not flow into the Pacific, as many had hoped. In 1682, Robert Cavelier, Sieur de La Salle, followed the same route and at the mouth of the Mississippi claimed "this country of Louisiana" for King Louis XIV.

La Salle had claimed a huge expanse of land, which later became known as the Louisiana territory. In his eyes, this entire region on the west of the Mississippi River was now ruled by the King of France. No mention was made of the many American Indian societies who were already living there at the time. Later, La Salle returned to the area by sea with the intention of establishing a fort at the mouth of the Mississippi, but he was unable to find it. After establishing a fort on the Texas coast, he led several

Henry Hudson's interaction with the first people of the Northeast was mostly very friendly. In this 19th-century painting, he invites a group of Indians onto his ship to trade furs.

The Vikings in North America

In 1003, Viking explorer Leif Eriksson landed at a place he called Vinland, now thought to have been on the North American coast. A colony was started, but it was abandoned due to trouble with the Indians. Many experts think that a site in Newfoundland contains the remains of the colony. Since the Viking sojourn had no effect on future settlement, it is usually regarded as a footnote.

unsuccessful marching expeditions in hope of finding the Mississippi. During one such expedition, he was killed by his own men. In 1688, the remaining colonists in the fort were killed by hostile Indians, who did not acknowledge the French right to their land.

La Salle was one of the first Europeans to explore the Mississippi River. This painting by George Catlin depicts him standing at the mouth of the river, surrounded by Indians, claiming the territory of Louisiana for France.

THE DUTCH

Although he was English by birth, explorer Henry Hudson was hired by the Dutch in 1609 to find a Northwest Passage to Asia. When he sailed up the river that now bears his name, the Indians he met were very friendly. The same was true when the Dutch established their colony of New Amsterdam on the island of Manhattan. But, as was the case in other regions, this early friendship was soon punctured by violence. By 1643, the settlers were fighting the tribes of the Wappinger Confederacy, located on the banks of the Hudson River. The conflict ended with the death of hundreds of Indians and a breakup of the confederacy.

THE ENGLISH IN NEW ENGLAND

Several years before the Pilgrims arrived in the Mayflower, English traders and explorers established friendly relations with the Indians along the New England coast. That changed suddenly when one of the English sea captains kidnapped several Indians to sell on the Mediterranean slave market. The resentment still smoldered when the Pilgrims landed in the area in 1620.

New England was given its name by English explorer John Smith, who created this map of the region in 1614. Smith's portrait appears in the corner.

THE SPANISH IN THE SOUTHWEST

Through the 16th and 17th centuries, the Spanish empire was very strong. The colonies of New Spain stretched from Mexico through much of South America. Their cities, with great cathedrals and universities, rivaled those of their European homeland. As conquistadors moved north into what is now New Mexico and Arizona, they hoped they could duplicate these achievements in North America.

CORONADO'S SEARCH

In 1539, Francisco de Coronado, governor of the Spanish province of Nueva Galicia on the Mexican coast, embarked on an expedition to present-day Arizona and New Mexico. Like de Soto in the Southeast, he was searching for the Seven Cities of Cíbola in the hope of obtaining treasure (see p.76). Unfortunately, these legendary golden cities didn't actually exist, and Coronado was frustrated from the beginning.

At first, he thought a pueblo belonging to the Zuni tribe might be one of the cities, but it turned out to be only "a little crowded village . . . crumpled all together." When the Spanish approached the pueblo, the Zuni people sprinkled sacred cornmeal across their path and warned the white men not to cross. The villagers also unleashed a shower of arrows onto Coronado's soldiers. In response, the Spaniards attacked the Indians and overran the pueblo with their horses and guns.

Although the Zuni village was not one of the golden cities, the Spanish soldiers under Coronado soon found that it was the center of a vast agricultural area, and the holding place for large stores of food. With winter quickly approaching, one of Coronado's men wrote: "We found something that we prized much more than gold or silver; namely maize (corn) and beans, turkeys larger than those in New Spain."

Coronado explored much of the American Southwest over the next few years. Although he traveled as far as present-day Kansas, he still found no evidence of the golden cities. Increasingly frustrated, the Spaniards burned several Pueblo villages, forcing the survivors to flee into the mountains.

In 1542, Coronado returned to Mexico. His failure to find any mineral wealth led Spanish gold seekers to avoid the Southwest for the next 40 years.

THE FIRST SPANISH COLONY IN THE SOUTHWEST

During the 1580s, several Catholic missionaries made excursions into the Southwest, bringing soldiers to protect them. Relations with the local tribes were generally peaceful. Then, in 1598, Spanish authorities in Mexico

Francisco de Coronado crosses the plains of Kansas, accompanied by his soldiers and an Indian guide, in a painting by Frederic Remington. At this stage, his chances of finding the legendary Seven Cities were beginning to look bleak.

launched a major migration. A large swath of the Southwest was declared to be a Spanish province, and was given the name New Mexico. The migration north was led by Juan de Oñate, governor of the new province. His instructions stated: "Your main purpose shall be the service of God Our Lord [and] the spreading of his holy Catholic faith [to] the natives of the . . . provinces."

Oñate's procession must have been an impressive sight: the governor, other officials, soldiers, and priests—all on horseback—followed by 400 settlers (including men, women, and children), along with 7,000 head of cattle and sheep, and nearly 100 wagons. The Pueblo people greeted the settlers with friendship and gifts.

Juan de Oñate left this inscription on a rock in New Mexico. It reads: "Passed by here, the Adelantado Don Juan de Oñate, from the discovery of the Sea of the South, the 16th day of April, 1605."

Forty years had passed since the cruelties of the Coronado expedition, and the Pueblos seemed willing to put the incident behind them. The Spanish, however, seemed to have learned nothing about getting along with North American Indians.

HEAVY-HANDED TACTICS

Governor Oñate displayed the arrogance of a conquistador when he ordered Pueblo villagers to give him control of their town, which he renamed San Juan and established as his capital. The people of the village were converted to Christianity. Most probably accepted the new faith only because they feared the black-robed friars.

Oñate's tactics finally ran into resistance at the Acoma Pueblo. When his lieutenant demanded food, water, and wood, the Acoma refused. They had previously given such items to the Spanish as gifts, but a demand for them was a different matter. They finally agreed to sell some corn to the Spanish, but when Oñate's lieutenant entered the Pueblo to collect, things turned violent. The lieutenant was killed along with a dozen of his soldiers.

THE TRAGEDY OF ACOMA

When Oñate learned that his men had been killed, he ordered a full-scale attack on the Pueblo. Equipped with muskets and cannons, the Spanish soldiers stormed the town. After days of fighting, in which more than 1,000 Acoma were killed, the Indians were forced to surrender.

Oñate then ordered vicious retribution to be doled out to the defeated Indians. All males over the age of 25 had one foot amputated and were sentenced to 20 years of slavery. These mutilations

Acoma Pueblo

Situated on a mesa rising nearly 400 feet (122 m) above the surrounding land, Acoma Pueblo is also known as Sky City. It is located west of present-day Albuquerque, New Mexico, and has been occupied for an estimated 1,000 years. Many experts think it is the oldest continually inhabited town in the United States.

were carried out in public to set an example. All Acomas between 12 and 25 were also condemned to slavery. Girls under 12 were turned over to the friars, and boys were turned over to the military. Two Hopi Indians who were visiting were sent home with their right hands cut off as a warning.

The Pueblo Indians had been beaten down by the Spaniards, but not defeated. Thousands moved into mountain hideaways, waiting until the time was right to launch a rebellion against the Spanish.

OÑATE'S BITTER END

Several years after Acoma, a Spanish court removed Oñate from office, stripped him of his honors, and fined him for his crimes of torture and mass enslavement. This was part of the Catholic Church's efforts to reverse the brutality of the conquistadors. Although many considered the Indians to be less than human and not endowed with souls, the church declared that they were to be regarded as fully human. This helped soften the brutality of the Spanish conquerors, but unfortunately it didn't stop them from taking over the Indians' native lands.

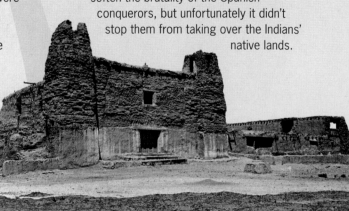

The mission church at Acoma Pueblo was built by the Spanish in 1629 and stands to this day. In the 1900s, it was falling into disrepair, but it has since been restored.

Acoma Pueblo is one of the oldest continually inhabited communities in the United States. Today, most residents still follow traditional ways of life.

ENCOUNTERS ON THE WEST COAST

Although the European conquest of North America generally moved from east to west, there were several early encounters on the West Coast. Spanish missionaries, Russian traders, and English and American explorers all visited the area before 1800. In one contact after another, the Indians welcomed the strangers in friendship.

THE SPANISH IN CALIFORNIA

In 1542, the same year that Coronado left the Southwest, Spanish explorer Juan Rodríguez Cabrillo sailed along the California coast. He landed at Catalina Island as well as the future sites of San Diego and other cities.

Although Cabrillo claimed California for Spain, the Spanish didn't start showing real interest in the region until 200 years later, when they began building missions. The primary purpose of these missions was to convert the local Indians to Christianity, but Spain hoped that they might also lead to an eventual Spanish colonization of the region. The first California mission was established at San Diego in 1769. Over the next 54 years, 20 more missions were built, largely the work of the legendary Father Junípero Serra. The chain of missions, all about a day's travel apart from each other, were connected by a road known as El Camino Real, meaning "the Royal Highway."

The missionaries strove not only to make the Indians accept the Christian faith, but to turn them into Spanish citizens who followed the European way of life. The Indians were often made to work on farms, a significant change for California's hunting-and-gathering tribes. The reactions of the Indians to the mission system varied considerably. Many seemed to accept the lifestyles imposed upon them by the Spanish, but there were also several violent

Missions were the center of Spanish activity in California. This illustration depicts priests, soldiers, and Indians outside of a mission church.

uprisings that took place along the California coast. These uprisings were always quickly suppressed by the superior military force of the Spanish.

Today, there is continuing debate about the treatment of the Indians under the Spanish missions. Certainly, they fared better than their neighbors in the Southwest, but it is also clear that the missions were responsible for the gradual decline in the native cultures of the region.

Fort Ross, in northern California, was Russia's southernmost American colony. Today, reconstructions of the major buildings, including this wooden church, have been built at the site.

RUSSIANS IN THE PACIFIC NORTHWEST

In 1725, Danish explorer Vitus Bering, sailing under the Russian flag, made a 6,000-mile (9,654 km) journey across Russia and Asia. When he reached the coast, he and his crew built a ship and continued exploring. Bering sailed north through the strait that now bears his name, which separates Siberia and Alaska. In the dense fog, he could not see the coastline of North America to the east, but he knew that it had to be nearby.

Bering tried again in 1741. This time he landed on Kayak and Southeast Islands, off the coast of Alaska. On his return, his ship was stranded by bad weather. Bering and 19 of his crewmen died, apparently of scurvy—a disease common among sailors, resulting from a deficiency of Vitamin C. The survivors built another ship and returned home.

Throughout Bering's wanderings, contacts with Indians were minimal, but they always

northern California. Eventually, competition with England and the United States led to a lessening of Russian interest. In addition, the Russians had enslaved many of the Alaskan Aleuts and they encountered increasingly violent opposition from the remaining Aleuts, as well as from the Tlingit and other tribes.

By 1800, the population of the Aleuts had declined by 90 percent, and the Tlingit continued to attack the Russian outposts. A few decades later, the Russians decided they'd had enough. In

The Columbia's Role in World Trade

Robert Gray and the *Columbia* played a key role in world trade. First, Gray's Boston-based crew traded with the Indians along the Northwest coast, exchanging beads, iron, hatchets, and other items for otter pelts. With a full hold, the *Columbia* then sailed to China, where the furs fetched higher prices than in Europe. Chinese merchants filled the ship with luxury items, such as tea, porcelain, and silk. Over the next 40 years, *Columbia* helped Boston become the center of the profitable China trade.

ship's captain, Robert Gray, named the river the Columbia. A few years later, President Thomas Jefferson sent an expedition, led by

The missionaries strove not only to make the Indians accept the Christian faith, but also to turn them into Spanish citizens.

seemed to be on friendly terms. Then, when Bering's crew arrived home, they were received as heroes—due not so much to their remarkable survival story, as to the sea-otter pelts they brought with them. Suddenly, Russians had a keen interest in trading for furs with the Indian tribes on the Northwest coast of North America. The demand for otter furs would soon be as high as the demand for beaver pelts.

Starting in 1750, more and more Russian ships appeared off the Northwest coast. Russian trading posts, protected by forts, soon dotted the coastline from Alaska to

William Clark joined Meriwether Lewis on a famous expedition in 1804.

1867, they sold Alaska to the United States, giving up their interests in the area.

ENGLISH AND AMERICANS

When the Declaration of Independence was signed in 1776, most Americans in the east had never heard of California or of Indians living in the Pacific Northwest. That began to change a few years later. In 1792, an American ship named the *Columbia* sailed into a bay in modern-day Oregon. A beautiful river emptied into the bay and the

Meriwether Lewis and William Clark, to explore the vast area of western land acquired from France in the Lousiana Purchase. Lewis and Clark traveled from the Mississippi River all the way to the Oregon coast. Along the way, their interactions with Native tribes were generally peaceful, and Indians often assisted the explorers on their quest. The most famous of these Indian guides was the Shoshoni woman, Sacajawea (see p.51).

Meanwhile, the English were expanding their influence as far as western Canada. They had entered the fur trade in 1670, when they formed the Hudson's Bay Company to compete with the French. By 1800, the company had forts across the continent. Unfortunately, the company sometimes traded liquor to the Indians—a widespread practice among white traders. The influx of alcohol caused severe damage to many Indian societies.

This Penobscot jacket shows heavy European influence, both in its use of beads and its tailored shape.

CHAPTER 4

THE EUROPEAN IMPACT

Indian societies change due to European influence

In the long run, the impact of European contact on Indian societies was devastating. Entire cultures were wiped out by violence and disease, and the survivors were forced onto reservations. At first, however, many tribes derived some benefits from the cultural exchange. Northwest societies amassed great wealth by trading with whites, and Plains tribes adopted a new way of life after the introduction of the horse. This chapter takes a look at how Indian people were affected in the continent's different culture regions, and how specific tribes changed—for the better and for the worse.

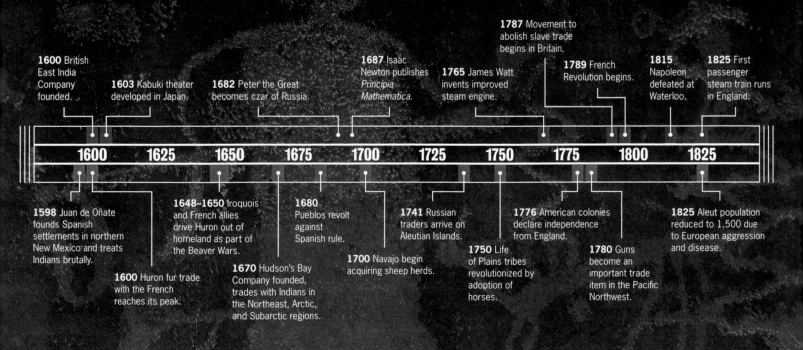

1787 Movement to abolish slave trade begins in Britain.

1600 British East India Company founded.

1603 Kabuki theater developed in Japan.

1682 Peter the Great becomes czar of Russia.

1687 Isaac Newton publishes *Principia Mathematica*.

1765 James Watt invents improved steam engine.

1789 French Revolution begins.

1815 Napoleon defeated at Waterloo.

1825 First passenger steam train runs in England.

| 1600 | 1625 | 1650 | 1675 | 1700 | 1725 | 1750 | 1775 | 1800 | 1825 |

1598 Juan de Oñate founds Spanish settlements in northern New Mexico and treats Indians brutally.

1600 Huron fur trade with the French reaches its peak.

1648–1650 Iroquois and French allies drive Huron out of homeland as part of the Beaver Wars.

1670 Hudson's Bay Company founded, trades with Indians in the Northeast, Arctic, and Subarctic regions.

1680 Pueblos revolt against Spanish rule.

1700 Navajo begin acquiring sheep herds.

1741 Russian traders arrive on Aleutian Islands.

1750 Life of Plains tribes revolutionized by adoption of horses.

1776 American colonies declare independence from England.

1780 Guns become an important trade item in the Pacific Northwest.

1825 Aleut population reduced to 1,500 due to European aggression and disease.

● Events in rest of world   ● Events in North America

CHANGES IN THE EAST

The experiences of the Northeast and Southeast people varied widely after the arrival of Europeans. Many tribes in Canada gained great wealth by trading furs with the French. However, many others had a more negative experience. In New England and Virginia, for example, uneasy friendship soon gave way to violent conflict. In addition, tribes in all areas suffered a massive population loss due to European diseases.

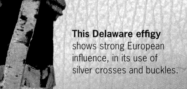

A REVOLUTIONARY TRADE

The Huron, Ojibwe, and other Indian nations in what is now Ontario, Canada, were at first amused and puzzled by the Europeans. When the newcomers offered them hard biscuits and wine as refreshment, the Huron joked that these strangers ate wood and drank blood. Soon, the Indians learned that, in exchange for beaver pelts, the French would trade them useful new tools—such as iron kettles that never wore out, colorful glass beads, or even awe-inspiring guns. By 1600, the Huron and others had established a flourishing trade with the French, which changed the Native economy in many ways, both good and bad. For example, although tribes became wealthy from the trade, they also became indebted to white traders, and friendly relations between neighboring tribes often gave way to fierce competition for pelts.

This Delaware effigy shows strong European influence, in its use of silver crosses and buckles.

The fur trade gave many Northeast tribes access to an unexpected material prosperity. Here, a group of Indians negotiates a trade on a European ship.

CONFLICT IN NEW ENGLAND

The Indian tribes in New England did not fare as well as their neighbors to the north. Starting with the arrival of the Pilgrims in 1620, thousands of English migrants relocated to the area, in what became known as the "Great Migration." Although the Indians initially maintained peaceful relations with the colonists, the increasing English population soon threatened to drive the Indians away from their ancestral lands. In the end, violent conflict became inevitable (see pp.120–121).

TROUBLE IN THE SOUTHEAST

The tribes in the Southeast also engaged in trade with the Spanish and English settlers. In this area, it was the skin of the white-tailed deer, rather than the beaver, that was the primary animal commodity. However, there was another commodity the Europeans sought in the region that was even more prized than hides: Indian slaves. Starting in the late 17th century, white traders aggressively encouraged Indians to take captives from neighboring tribes, who could then be sold as slaves. The disruption to traditional ways of life was profound.

THE POWHATAN

When the English established Jamestown in 1607, they were met by Indians of the powerful Powhatan Confederacy. The Confederacy was an alliance of about 100 villages with a population of more than 9,000. The Powhatan chief wasn't sure how to deal with the strangers. At first he encouraged his people to give them food and teach them how to grow the local crops, deciding it was better for his people to maintain peace. As in New England, however, this peace would turn out to be temporary, and the Powhatan would soon be fighting for their lives (see pp.118–119).

The Powhatans lived in Virginia, but were part of the Northeast culture area. This engraving depicts the chief in his longhouse.

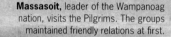

The white-tail deer had a hide that could be sold for a high price in Europe. It was used to make elegant gloves, bookbindings, and other luxury goods

Massasoit, leader of the Wampanoag nation, visits the Pilgrims. The groups maintained friendly relations at first.

THE HURON

In the mid-1500s, the Huron started trading furs with the French. This trade grew rapidly, reaching a peak in the early 1600s. The life of the people in every village came to be centered on the furs—catching the beaver, preparing the skins, and making use of the items they got in return.

A NEW PROSPERITY

The furs brought the Huron a new age of prosperity. The men enjoyed the increased hunting and trapping. In addition to providing greater incentive for these activities, the fur trade also provided them with tools that made the work easier, such as steel knives and traps. Similarly, the women found that preparing the pelts was faster with the new European-style tools.

The new trade goods added ease and creativity to many other tasks as well. Glass beads, for example, were colorful and easy to sew onto garments, moccasins, bags, and other items. Huron women took delight in arranging the beads in intricate new designs. European cotton cloth was also highly prized—it was colorful and much easier to cut and sew than deerskin.

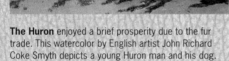

The Huron enjoyed a brief prosperity due to the fur trade. This watercolor by English artist John Richard Coke Smyth depicts a young Huron man and his dog.

ENDANGERED SPECIES

The Huron villages were scattered across the fertile woodlands of southern Ontario, where the supply of beavers seemed practically limitless. Unfortunately, it wasn't. In the past, all Indian societies had been careful not to kill more animals than they needed. By the mid-1600s, however, the pressure to provide more and more pelts led to a steady decline in beaver populations across the Northeast. Neighboring tribes that had once been on good terms were now competing, and sometimes fighting, over furs.

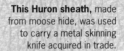

This Huron sheath, made from moose hide, was used to carry a metal skinning knife acquired in trade.

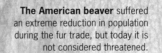

The American beaver suffered an extreme reduction in population during the fur trade, but today it is not considered threatened.

A VULNERABLE POSITION

The Huron derived many benefits from the fur trade, but their position at the top was precarious. Some of the Iroquois tribes, who lived to the southeast in modern New York State, wanted to cut into the Huron trade, and they were willing to go to war for it. The Mohawk and the Seneca were the most aggressive. The Huron, however, were not in a strong position for war, even the brief raids that were the most common form of Indian warfare. One problem was that they had been decimated by disease when a smallpox epidemic raced through the villages near the Great Lakes. By 1650, the disease had reduced the Huron population from 30,000–40,000 to an estimated 10,000. Entire villages had been emptied by the deadly disease. The second problem was that the Mohawk were the only Indian nation that had traded for European guns. Researchers estimate that in 1650 the Mohawk had about 300 firearms, a powerful armory at a time when few other Indian nations possessed guns.

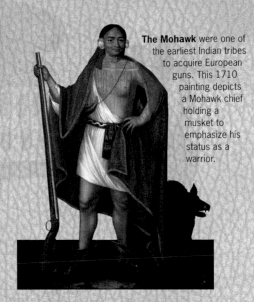

The Mohawk were one of the earliest Indian tribes to acquire European guns. This 1710 painting depicts a Mohawk chief holding a musket to emphasize his status as a warrior.

THE BEAVER WARS

In 1650, the Iroquois launched a surprise attack on the Huron. More than 1,000 warriors stormed through the villages, burning the longhouses and driving the survivors into the forests. Although the conflict, known as the Beaver Wars, would expand to involve the French, the English, and other Indian tribes, the Huron were effectively put out of the trading game by this one devastating attack.

The battle lines of the Beaver Wars were drawn decades earlier, when the French formed an alliance with the Huron and other tribes against the Iroquois. This engraving depicts an early conflict in 1609.

This Methodist mission was built in 1823 to serve the Huron who settled in Ohio. Indians of all tribes have often had to contend with Christians eager to convert them.

THE SCATTERING OF THE HURON NATION

After their defeat at the hands of the Iroquois, the Huron fled in different directions throughout the Great Lakes region and the St. Lawrence River Valley. Some settled around Quebec, where the government eventually set aside land as a reservation. But most Huron, now called the Wyandot, wandered in small bands, often accompanied by smaller tribes. They suffered terribly, often dying of starvation. The wandering continued into the 1700s as the Wyandot made their way for short periods into present-day Wisconsin, Minnesota, and Michigan. Some settled in Ohio. Throughout this period, Wyandot warriors joined with larger tribes whenever they had the chance, in order to fight the Iroquois or the American colonists, who were pushing farther west into Indian lands. Ultimately, this battle against the encroaching colonists was a battle the Huron and their allies couldn't win. In the 19th century, the Ohio Wyandot relocated to Oklahoma, where they are today known as the Wyandotte Nation.

INDIANS WERE FIRST

America's first people adopted many new ways of life from the European settlers. However, this cultural exchange was actually a two-way street. These pages provide a sampling of the many foods, artworks, and technologies that originated in pre-colonial North America and ended up spreading throughout the world.

FOOD

Turkey
Turkeys were hunted and domesticated in many regions.

Strawberries
The Iroquois cultivated these woodland berries in beds.

Mint
Some tribes used mint as a flavoring and a medicine.

Cacao
The plant that gives us chocolate was first grown by Mesoamericans.

Sunflower seeds
Indians used the sunflower for food, hair oil, dyes, and more.

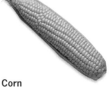

Corn
Maize was an important part of the culture of most farming tribes.

Venison
Deer were hunted for their meat and hides in many areas.

Peppers
Like chocolate, peppers may have reached the Southwest through trade with Mesoamerica.

Popcorn
Indians brought popcorn to the "First Thanksgiving" at Plymouth.

Lima beans
Lima beans were a key ingredient in succotash.

Green beans
These beans were a common crop throughout North America.

Pecans
Tribes in the East made various pecan dishes, including a nutritious "milk."

Maple syrup
Northeast Indians made syrup from the sap of maple trees.

Pumpkins
Pumpkins are a form of squash, one of the Indian "three sisters."

Jerky
This dried meat is now a popular snack across the United States.

Cranberries
Cranberries were an important ingredient in the spiced jerky known as pemmican.

Wild rice
Northeast Indians harvested this water-loving grain from canoes.

Kidney beans
This variety of bean is now used in dishes throughout the world.

Blueberries
Explorers saw the Huron harvest blueberries in the 1600s.

MEDICINES

Echinacea
The Plains Indians used this herb to treat colds and other ailments.

Cascara
Indians on the West Coast used this bark as a laxative.

Goldenseal
This root was used by some tribes as a health tonic and a dye.

ARTS AND CRAFTS

Northwest wood carvings
The wood carvings of the Northwest tribes show exquisite form and technique.

Navajo blankets
These woven blankets are prized for their geometric patterns.

Dreamcatchers
These Ojibwe dream filters now hang in many non-Indian homes.

Turquoise jewelry
The silver-and-turquoise jewelry developed by the Navajo is now popular across the Southwest.

CLOTHING

Moccasins
This comfortable footwear enjoys an ongoing popularity.

Parkas
The influence of these Inuit coats can still be felt in modern cold-weather jackets.

Snowshoes
These useful webbed shoes were developed by tribes of the Arctic and Subarctic.

SPORTS AND RECREATION

Kayaks
The first kayaks were hunting boats made by the Inuit.

Toboggans
People of the Subarctic used these sleds to haul goods over snowy terrain.

Dogsleds
The Inuit used dogsleds for long trips and hunting expeditions.

Lacrosse
This Native American sport is now popular around the world.

CHANGES ON THE PLAINS

Contact with Europeans brought revolutionary changes to the Native way of life on the Great Plains. Of all the changes, none were more dramatic than the introduction of the horse. Tribes with horses—including the Sioux, Comanche, Arapaho, and Pawnee—adopted a new way of life that was exciting and fast-paced. Unfortunately, as was the case with all Indian tribes, this golden age was temporary, and the people of the Great Plains would eventually be forced onto reservations against their will.

A horse-drawn travois could be much larger, and carry much more weight, than one drawn by a dog, as was traditional before European contact.

A HORSE BY ANY OTHER NAME

Many groups we now think of as Plains tribes didn't move into the area until after the horse had become a part of their lives, having been forced to move west due to colonization in the East. Since the only domesticated animal they had known previously was the dog, many tribes gave horses names related to their word for dog. The Cree called them *mistatim*, meaning "big dog," and the Comanche used nouns that translated as "medicine dog," "good dog," and "mysterious dog."

Taming a horse could be a difficult business. One method used by the Plains cultures involved having a boy ride the horse while a man held it by a roper, or tether.

Buffalo Hunting

1875 Luther Standing Bear was an Oglala Sioux and the author of several books. In *My People, The Sioux* he describes his first buffalo hunt, which took place on horseback.

At the top of the hill, all the hunters turned their horses loose, and the animals started in running like the wind! I whipped up my little black mare and nearly got ahead of the others. Soon I was mixed up in the dust and could see nothing ahead of me. All I could hear was the roar and rattle of the hoofs of the buffalo as they thundered along. My pony shied this way and that, and I had to hold on for dear life.

For a time I did not even try to pull an arrow from my quiver, as I had all I could do to take care of myself. I knew if my pony went down and one of those big animals stepped on me, it would be my last day on earth . . .

I rode right up alongside the buffalo, just as my father had instructed me. Drawing an arrow from my quiver, and holding to my pony with all the strength of my legs, I fitted the arrow and let drive with all my strength. I had expected to kill the buffalo right quick, but the arrow went into the neck—and I thought I had taken such good aim! But the buffalo only shook her head and kept on running. I again caught up with her, and let another arrow loose, which struck near the heart.

[After] I shot my fourth arrow into her . . . she staggered and dropped over on her side, and was soon dead. So I had killed my first buffalo.

HORSE TRAINING

As time went by, Plains cultures developed different methods of training horses. The Cheyenne in particular were regarded as outstanding breeders and trainers of horses. Cheyenne boys used a special method to break, or tame, a wild horse: They simply talked softly to the horse, singing and petting. Other tribes used more direct methods involving force.

Women's saddlebags were made in pairs to hang on either side of a saddle. This example includes the image of a horse, made with porcupine quills.

A NEW WAY OF LIFE

Hunting bison on horseback was very different from hunting them on foot. Instead of a family's plodding search for a small herd, men and older boys now enjoyed the sport of riding at a gallop alongside a stampeding herd. One or two well-placed arrows would bring down the animal that had been selected. Fortunately, there were plenty of bison for these high-speed hunts. It is estimated that at least 30 million of the shaggy beasts roamed the Plains in the late 1700s, roaming as far East as present-day New York, Pennsylvania, and Virginia. Some estimates run as high as 60 million. These huge herds combined with skilled hunters on horseback gave the Plains tribes plenty of food, hides, and materials for making tools and weapons. Always consious of their relationship to their environment, however, they continued to place limits on how many bison a village could kill.

A skilled hunter could kill a buffalo with a single arrow. In this Catlin painting, a rider takes aim at his prey.

The life of the Sioux changed in many ways with the addition of horses. They entered an era that was prosperous, exciting—and all too short. With the added power of horses, they could now take more material goods with them as they roamed across the plains, and their portable tipis nearly doubled in size.

Larger tipis and European-style tools were only some of the benefits of the Sioux's new lifestyle.

BIGGER TIPIS

When the Sioux first moved onto the Great Plains, their tipis were limited to about 8 feet (2.4 m) in diameter, because a dog-pulled travois could drag only about 75 pounds (34 kg) of buffalo-hide tent. Since a horse could haul hundreds of pounds, the diameter could now be 15 feet (4.6 m). As before, the Sioux often decorated the outside walls of their tipis with pictographs, but now they had a larger canvas to work with.

This Dakota Sioux saddle is made from tanned hide stuffed with fur.

A SOFTER RIDE

Like other Plains tribes, the Sioux originally rode horses bareback, without a saddle. Over time, however, they began to use saddles and stirrups more frequently, since they provided better stability and control. Still, the Sioux "pad saddle" was simpler than its European counterpart. It had hardly any cantle to support the rider's back and had no pommel on the front to hold onto. Stirrups were usually made of wood and attached by a rawhide strap.

WAR ON THE GO

With the introduction of horses, the work of hunting became more sport than work for the Sioux men. This gave them more free time for working on crafts and for their favorite pastime—warfare. As always, war provided the path to honor and prestige, but now that they had horses, they had to adapt their strategies to their new mode of transportation. Even on horseback, however, the wars of the Sioux and neighboring tribes were relatively small, with a great emphasis on counting coup. As it happened, horses came in handy in this regard as well: Among the Sioux, and several other Plains tribes, a favorite way of counting coup was to steal a prize horse or two from an enemy.

Roomier Lodgings

1832 American artist George Catlin, who visited Sioux villages in the 1830s, described the comfort of the larger tent made possible by the horse.

Inside of these tents, the fire is placed in the center, the smoke escaping out at the top; and at night, everyone sleeps . . . with their feet to the fire, a most safe, and not uncomfortable mode. To enter . . . you have to stoop rather awkwardly, but when you are in, you find a lofty space of some 20 feet above your head. . . . You see shields, and quivers, and lances, and saddles, and medicine bags, and pouches, and spears, and cradles, and buffalo masks (which each man keeps for dancing the buffalo dance), and a great variety of other picturesque things hanging suspended from the poles of the tent, to which they are fastened by thongs; the whole presenting, with the picturesque group around the fire, one of the most [unusual] scenes imaginable.

Two Sioux warriors on horseback look into the distance in this photograph, thought to have been taken around 1899.

ALL DECKED OUT

With the introduction of beads from the Europeans, the ceremonial dress of the Sioux became more elaborate. This included the traditional feathered headdresses, or war bonnets, which could be worn only by proven warriors. Despite depictions in popular culture, these types of headdresses were worn only during wars or special ceremonies. They were not a part of the Sioux's everyday costume, which was relatively practical and plain.

Ceremonial dress marked the status of an elder. This statue of a Sioux chief is wearing a headdress, a poncho-style shirt, and moccasins decorated with porcupine quills.

To see how the Sioux lived before contact with Europeans, see pp.44–45.

WEAPONS OF THE PLAINS

During the period of Euro-American conquest, the Indians of the Great Plains used both traditional weapons and firearms introduced from the east. The white settlers and soldiers used guns almost exclusively. These pages look at the weapons used on the Plains over the years—by both Indians and non-Indians. In addition to warfare, many of these weapons were used for hunting and self-defense.

NEW WEAPONS

Rifle musket
With early rifles, a new bullet was inserted at the end of the barrel after each shot. A Native marksman could shoot four or five arrows in the time it took to load and shoot this gun once.

Springfield Model 1873 "Trapdoor" Rifle
A breech-loading rifle was reloaded from the breech, or rear, of the gun, reducing the time between shots. The Springfield was used extensively by the U.S. Army against the Indians, and was also a favorite of Geronimo.

Winchester Model 1873 Rifle
Known as "the gun that won the West," the Winchester was a repeating rifle, meaning that multiple shots could be fired without having to reload.

Indian rifle
Although Indians did not make their own guns, they did sometimes decorate them with painted animal skins, as shown here.

Colt revolver
The "six shooter" held six bullets in a revolving chamber. It was designed for the army, but soon became popular with civilians, especially in the west.

.44-40 Winchester cartridge
A cartridge held a bullet and gunpowder, eliminating the need to load the powder separately.

Coup stick
A coup stick was used to touch an enemy warrior and then run away unharmed, thus increasing one's status.

Bow and arrows
Many tribes preferred hunting with bows even after the introduction of guns.

War club
A club was a primitive weapon, but still useful in hand-to-hand combat. It could also be used to deal a fatal blow to a wounded animal.

Long-handled club
After they acquired horses, Plains tribes started making clubs with longer handles so they could be easily used on horseback.

Lance
Officers of Plains warrior societies used lances in both ceremonies and battles.

Decorated club
Some clubs were highly decorated according to the warrior's taste. They were used for both practical and ceremonial purposes.

Tomahawk
Tomahawks originally featured stone heads, but after European contact, metal heads became more common. They were used as weapons and all-purpose tools.

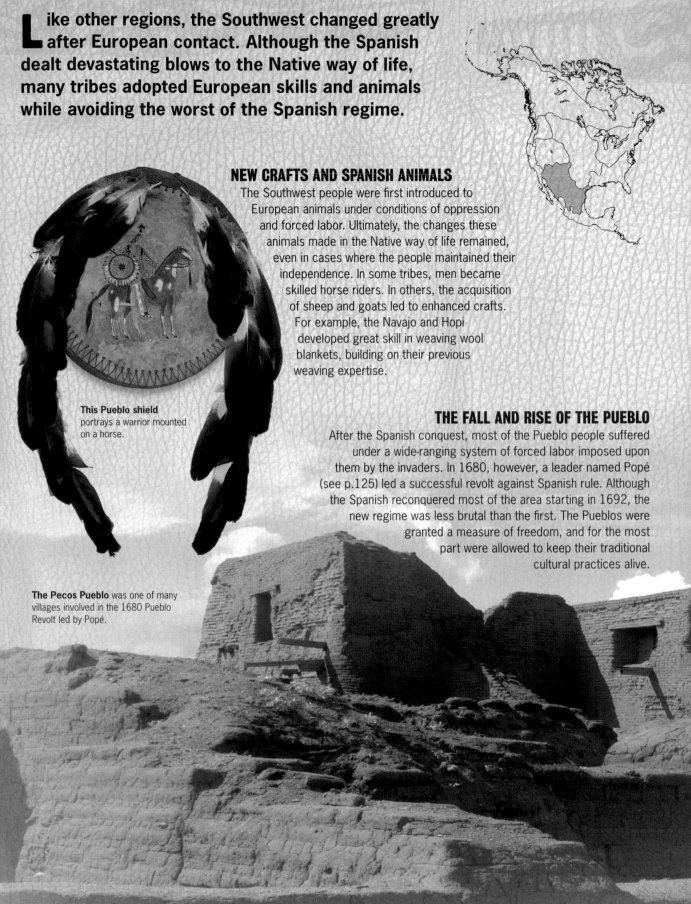

Like other regions, the Southwest changed greatly after European contact. Although the Spanish dealt devastating blows to the Native way of life, many tribes adopted European skills and animals while avoiding the worst of the Spanish regime.

NEW CRAFTS AND SPANISH ANIMALS

The Southwest people were first introduced to European animals under conditions of oppression and forced labor. Ultimately, the changes these animals made in the Native way of life remained, even in cases where the people maintained their independence. In some tribes, men became skilled horse riders. In others, the acquisition of sheep and goats led to enhanced crafts. For example, the Navajo and Hopi developed great skill in weaving wool blankets, building on their previous weaving expertise.

This Pueblo shield portrays a warrior mounted on a horse.

THE FALL AND RISE OF THE PUEBLO

After the Spanish conquest, most of the Pueblo people suffered under a wide-ranging system of forced labor imposed upon them by the invaders. In 1680, however, a leader named Popé (see p.125) led a successful revolt against Spanish rule. Although the Spanish reconquered most of the area starting in 1692, the new regime was less brutal than the first. The Pueblos were granted a measure of freedom, and for the most part were allowed to keep their traditional cultural practices alive.

The Pecos Pueblo was one of many villages involved in the 1680 Pueblo Revolt led by Popé.

A Shift in Power

The Spanish influence in the Southwest began to lessen after 1821. In that year, the people of Mexico revolted against their Spanish rulers and succeeded in winning their independence. Twenty-five years later, in 1846, Mexico fought a two-year war against the United States. The American victory forced Mexico to surrender all of its land north of the Rio Grande into U.S. hands. This territory included all of modern-day Arizona, New Mexico, Colorado, Utah, and parts of Nevada and Wyoming. From that time on, the Southwest Indians faced white Americans and the U.S. Army, rather than Spanish forces, in their struggle to save their lands and their way of life.

APACHE RAIDERS

The Apache were unusual in many ways. Although they did acquire horses, their warriors and hunters preferred running to riding. They were very rugged people, and could run for hours without tiring. When the Spanish moved into the Southwest, the Apache began conducting raids on their settlements, which grew increasingly intense over time. These raids involved stealing food, horses, and even Pueblo people, who were sold on the widespread slave market in the area.

The Apache were an athletic people who liked to travel on foot, as demonstrated by this Apache man near Black River, Arizona.

INDEPENDENT PEOPLE

The Navajo had already learned to become outstanding farmers under the influence of the Pueblos. When the Spanish arrived, they also learned to raise sheep and goats, which led to the development of their famous wool blankets. Unlike their Pueblo neighbors, the Navajo were never conquered by the Spanish, although they did engage in occasional conflicts with the Spanish regime, and the two groups often competed for land. Due to a combination of good fortune and defensive skill, the Navajo managed to maintain their independence for 200 years after the Spanish first moved in.

Navajo blankets are known for their bright colors and striking geometric patterns.

THE NAVAJO

AFTER EUROPEAN CONTACT

While the Pueblos bore the brunt of Spanish oppression, the Navajo maintained control of their lands until the mid-1850s, when they started to be forced out by the United States. During this time, the Navajo became skilled at weaving beautiful wool blankets. Later, they also became experts at crafting silver jewelry. Although they were not developed until relatively late, these crafts remain popular to this day.

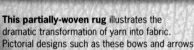

This partially-woven rug illustrates the dramatic transformation of yarn into fabric. Pictorial designs such as these bows and arrows were encouraged by white merchants.

MASTER WEAVERS

Probably the most striking new development in the life of the Navajo was their adoption of wool and weaving. Their neighbors, the Pueblos, had been weaving with cotton for hundreds of years. When the Spanish introduced sheep to the region, the Pueblos began weaving with wool—and the Navajo soon adopted the practice as well. The Navajo weaving process begins when the men and women shear the sheep. Then the women take over, washing the wool, combing it, and spinning it on a spindle to produce one long thread. The actual weaving is accomplished on an upright wooden loom, and is a long, slow task. Weaving for about 200 hours will produce a very small blanket. The genius of the Navajo women is in the patterns they create, some of which have special meanings. For example, layers of thick lines represent clouds and zig-zag patterns represent lightning. Other patterns were introduced by white traders, who gave the Navajo Persian designs to copy. Most of the woven pieces are used as blankets or wall hangings. Smaller ones are worn as shawls or ponchos.

Navajo weaving skills are passed down from mother to daughter. Here, two women weave on a loom while a flock of sheep passes on a ledge.

To see how the Navajo lived before contact with Europeans, see pp.38–39.

SILVER JEWELRY

The Navajo are famous for their outstanding silver-and-turquoise jewelry. In the mid-1800s, the U.S. government sent Colonel Henry Dodge to act as an agent for the Navajo. Dodge brought a Mexican silversmith, who taught his craft to the Navajo men and a few interested women. The Navajo were already skilled in working with stones, especially turquoise and coral. They now combined these stones with silver to produce magnificent bracelets, necklaces, and belt buckles. Like the Navajo weavings, these items commanded a high price from Spanish, Americans, and even the leaders of other tribes. Their reputation for great artistry continues in the 21st century.

Turquoise is a blue-green mineral that has been mined by cultures around the world since ancient times. Here, it is used in two Navajo rings.

This Navajo necklace incorporates 18 turquoise stones, inlaid in a silver chain, with a bridle-shaped *naja* at the bottom.

CHANGING TIMES

Everyone in Navajo society was affected by the European influence, not only weavers and jewelry makers. Even children changed their way of life in the new golden age. Boys, for example, learned to herd sheep and cattle, and to train horses. Girls learned to spin, dye, and weave wool, as preparation for womanhood. They also made clothing out of cotton, a fabric more suitable for the hot days of the Southwest than wool. Men and boys also borrowed clothing styles from other cultures—the Pueblos, the Spanish, Mexicans, and, later, the Americans. In the mid-1800s, they began draping a Navajo blanket over one shoulder, in the Mexican style. During this same period, Navajo women created distinctive velveteen blouses and full calico skirts, using cloth acquired from traders. These clothing styles are still popular today.

Navajo children participated in the new cultural practices along with their parents. Here, a pair of young Navajo girls tend to a flock of sheep in winter. Traditionally, it was more common for this role to be filled by boys.

Hopi girls display a Navajo blanket on the steps of their pueblo. Their squash-blossom hairstyles represent maturity and readiness for marriage.

HOPI NEIGHBORS

Like other tribes, the Hopi were determined to preserve their way of life, especially their religious practices and ceremonies. Unlike most others, they had the Navajo acting as a buffer between themselves and the Spanish. After the Pueblo Revolt of 1680, the Navajo were located between the Hopi villages and the remaining Spanish settlements. Coupled with active Hopi resistance, this prevented the Spanish from re-establishing a presence in the region, enabling the Hopi to take advantage of what the Spanish brought without losing their independence. Like the Navajo, the Hopi adopted began weaving with wool and making silver jewelry during this time. Through good luck and determination, they were able to enjoy a period of peace, independence, and prosperity.

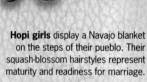

Navajo sandpaintings are created and destroyed in a single day, as part of a healing ceremony.

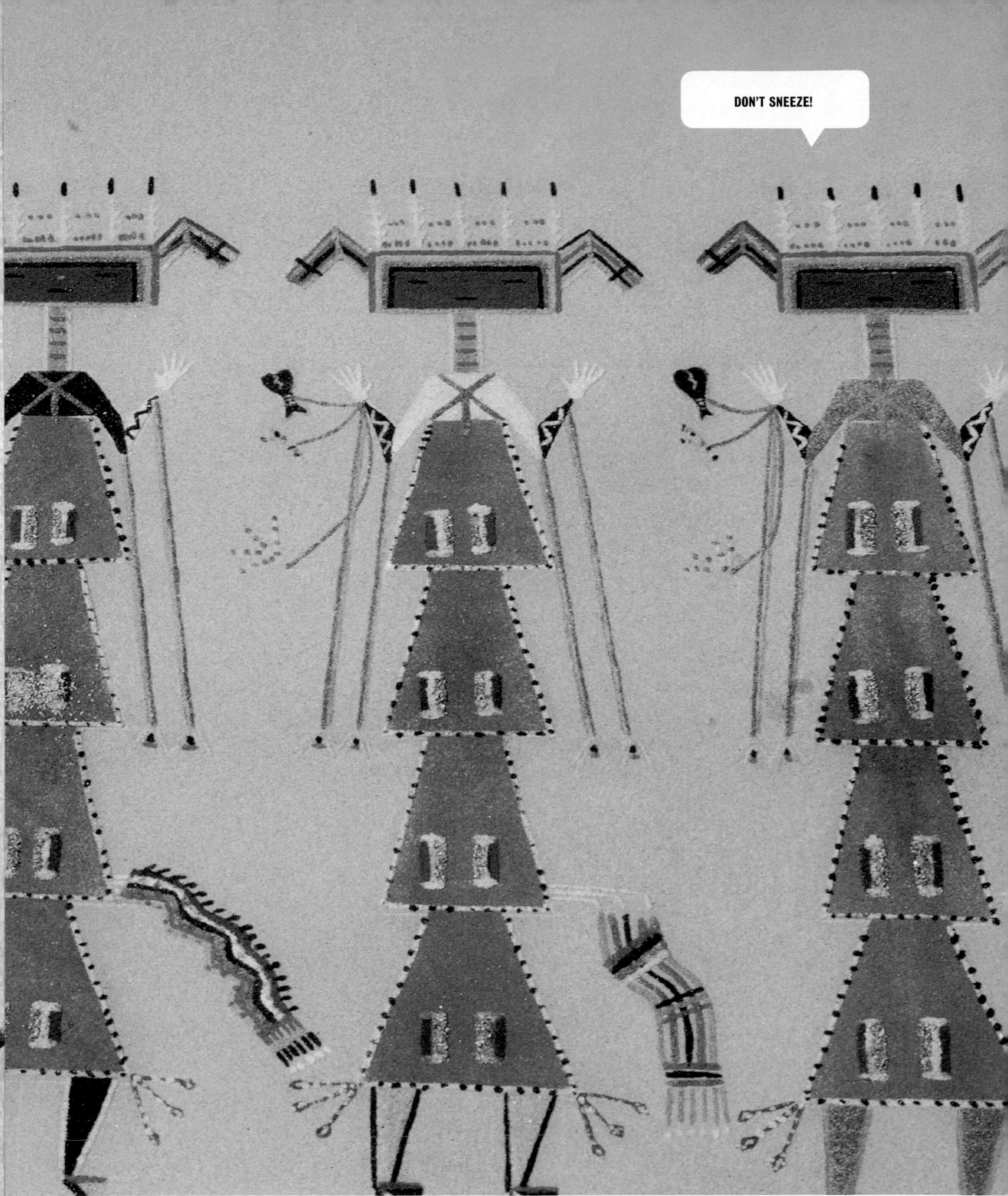
DON'T SNEEZE!

CHANGES IN THE NORTHWEST

British, American, and Russian traders discovered the riches of the Pacific Northwest at roughly the same time, in the mid- to late 1700s. Once they started trading with the newcomers, the local tribes enjoyed an extaordinary increase in material wealth. Unfortunately, the very success of the trade carried with it the seeds of disaster.

RICHES ON TOP OF RICHES

When Europeans and Americans first made contact with the Northwest Coast Indians, most tribes already lived in the midst of great material abundance. They had more than enough blankets, canoes, wood carvings, and even slaves. When the white traders began doing business with them, this wealth only increased. A common scene in one harbor after another was that of a European or American trading ship surrounded by dozens of canoes filled with Native people, who held up salmon and otter pelts. In exchange, the Indians received glass beads and all kinds of metal items—kettles, knives, and a variety of carpentry and woodworking tools. There were now many more sources of wealth and the Indians acquired them eagerly. With new, more efficient tools, daily tasks went more swiftly. This was particularly true of time-consuming projects such as building a long dugout canoe or a cedar plank house. The tribes could now devote more time to crafts such as carving totem poles.

This Tlingit fighting knife was made using iron acquired from trade.

Potlatches, such as this Tlingit gathering, allowed tribe members to show off their material wealth.

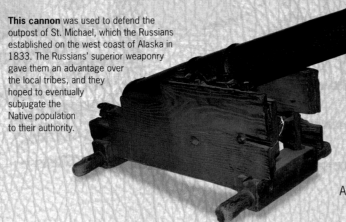

This cannon was used to defend the outpost of St. Michael, which the Russians established on the west coast of Alaska in 1833. The Russians' superior weaponry gave them an advantage over the local tribes, and they hoped to eventually subjugate the Native population to their authority.

CONFLICTS WITH THE RUSSIANS

The coastal people regarded the Russians as the most ruthless of the trading countries. At first, the two cultures engaged in friendly relations. Then, starting in 1800, the Russians began demanding tribute in the form of furs, offering nothing in return. The Tlingit put up a fierce resistance. At one point, they attacked the Russian settlement on Sitka Island with a large force and held the position for two years. The Tlingit would continue to launch small raids on the Russians until Alaska was sold to the United States in 1867.

GUNS AND GAME

In the late 18th century, guns became an important trade item in the Northwest, and for a time, they added to the great abundance that the coastal tribes enjoyed. With guns, hunters could greatly increase the number of sea otter, seals, and other wildlife they offered in trade. However, since individuals, families, and villages were in constant competition, they were soon killing far more animals than they needed. They were losing sight of the great Native American environmental ethic—to harvest only as many animals or plants as they needed. The result was a steady and rapid decline in the sea otter population. By the early 1800s, a species that had been plentiful had become relatively scarce and, by 1900, it was close to extinction.

Sea otters can spend their entire lives in the ocean. Since 1900, their population has rebounded due to conservation efforts.

Sweathouses were sometimes used by Northwest Indians in an attempt to cure smallpox and other European diseases. These traditional remedies did not meet with much success.

EUROPEAN DISEASES

Although the Europeans brought many valuable trade items to the Northwest, they also brought many diseases. When British explorer George Vancouver arrived on the beaches of Puget Sound, near present-day Seattle, in 1792, he found beaches littered with the remains of dozens of Indian smallpox victims. "The survivors were most terribly pitted . . ." a sailor reported. "Indeed many had lost their eyes." During this period, smallpox and other diseases spread up and down the coast, frequently wiping out entire villages. In California, the Pomo Indians, who were forced to work at Russia's Fort Ross, attempted to revolt against the Russians, but they had been so badly weakened by European diseases they coudln't put up much resistance.

THE HAIDA

AFTER EUROPEAN CONTACT

Like other Northwest Coast tribes, the Haida welcomed the exchange of goods with Europeans and Americans. The trade ushered in a burst of prosperity and a great artistic flowering, characterized by intricately carved pieces of woodwork. This period lasted about 100 years. After that time, the Haida gradually saw their fortunes begin to decline.

TOTEM POLES FOR ALL

Before the Haida began trading with Europeans, totem poles had been rare and required exhaustive labor. With metal tools, the artform really took off. In the past, men had worked with tools made of horn, bone, stone, and even beaver teeth. The steel tools provided by the Europeans were much better at carving. Totem poles became larger by the late 1700s, much more numerous, and more brightly colored. By making deep cuts in the wood and using bright colors, the carver achieved a dramatic effect. The poles had no religious purpose, but served instead to display the family's crest or history. While a main pole stood at the entrance to the family home, others were scattered around the village and in the graveyard.

Totem poles were once few and far between in Haida villages. By the time this photo was taken in 1884, they dominated the town.

This shaman's rattle is in the form of a hawk. Steel tools allowed the Haida to give wooden objects more detail and definition.

WOODEN WONDERS

The Haida used their new metal tools for more than just totem poles. Steel chisels, adzes, knives, and other items made woodworking so easy that the quality and number of all wood items was increased. These included masks, sculptures, and instruments, many of which were used in spiritual ceremonies.

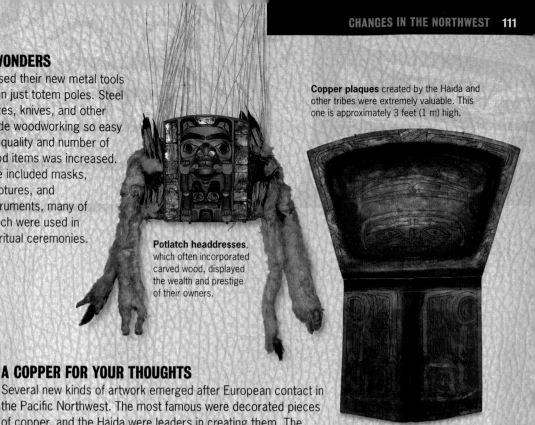

Potlatch headdresses, which often incorporated carved wood, displayed the wealth and prestige of their owners.

Copper plaques created by the Haida and other tribes were extremely valuable. This one is approximately 3 feet (1 m) high.

A COPPER FOR YOUR THOUGHTS

Several new kinds of artwork emerged after European contact in the Pacific Northwest. The most famous were decorated pieces of copper, and the Haida were leaders in creating them. The tribe acquired thin sheets of copper in trade or took them from wrecked sailing ships, which often used the metal to protect the bottom of the boat. The Haida artists then hammered or engraved these pieces of copper into beautiful designs. These "coppers" were in great demand and could be traded for more than 1,000 blankets.

TIME TO RELAX

With their increased prosperity, the Haida began to have more access to leisure time, especially during the long, cold winter. Leisure actvities enjoyed by the Haida and neigboring tribes might have included sharing a feast with a large group of villagers or taking a long canoe trip to visit relatives. A favorite form of leisure involved building a thatched hut over a quiet pool in a river. Six or more tribe members would sit on benches in the hut, with their feet and legs in the water. Others, on the bank, would then drop heated rocks into the pool, creating huge clouds of steam. The steam bath, which included rub downs with branches, was followed by a plunge into the cold river.

A group of Haidas pose outside the chief's house in the village of Masset, on Queen Charlotte's Island.

To see how the Haida lived before European contact, see pp.56–57.

THE KWAKWAKA'WAKW

In most Native societies, people did not think in terms of piling up wealth. The tribes of the Pacific Northwest were the exception to this rule—and the Kwakwaka'wakw [KWA-kwa-ka-wack] were perhaps the most extreme. They devoted much of their energy to acquiring wealth, and then giving it away or destroying it in potlatch ceremonies. Once trade with Europeans began, these ceremonies only became more extravagant.

Ceremonial slave killers were occasionally used to take the lives of Kwakwaka'wakw slaves during potlatches.

STATUS SYMBOLS

The potlatch was the most prominent feature of life among the Kwakwaka'wakw. For the owner of property, it meant the all-important chance to gain status and prestige. A potlatch was usually planned to celebrate an important event, such as a marriage or the naming of an heir. It could also be a means of overcoming some personal humiliation. The goal was to show one's greatness by giving away wealth, or by making a dramatic display of destroying it. For example, the host of a potlatch might give away his house, or burn it down; hand out piles of blankets or reduce them to ash. The more wealth he could get rid of, the greater the increase in his status.

HAVES AND HAVE NOTS

Although most Indian societies were fairly democratic, the Kwakwaka'wakw and other Northwest tribes had a rigid caste system. The men with wealth were the chiefs and nobles; others were commoners or slaves. In fact, slave ownership was an important form of wealth, and this led to frequent raids to capture slaves. Slaves might stay with an owner for life. They also could be traded, sold, or killed on a whim.

Two canoes pull ashore in a Kwakwaka'wakw wedding ceremony. A wedding was often used as an occasion to hold a potlatch.

SECRET SOCIETIES AND PERFORMANCES

Secret societies were an important part of Kwakwaka'wakw culture, along with that of their neighbors, the Nuu-chah-nulth. Although initiation into the societies did indeed take place under a cloak of secrecy, the main purpose of the groups was to stage elaborate public performances. The chiefs of the societies also had first choice in hosting potlatches. The Kwakwaka'wakw societies had names such as Grizzly Bear, Crazy Man, and Warrior, but the Cannibal Society was the most important. The performances put on by these societies involved many props, such as masks, puppets, and shields. After contact with Europeans, Northwest craftsmen used steel tools to reach new heights in the artistry of these props. A major difference between the performances of the Nuu-chah-nulth and the Kwakwaka'wakw was that the former emphasized humor while the latter stressed drama and violence.

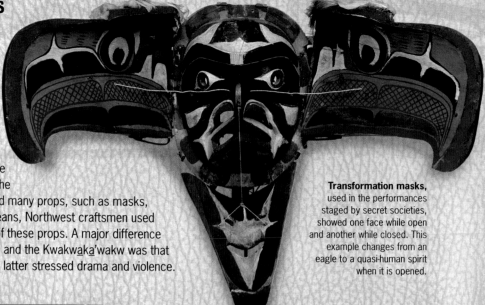

Transformation masks, used in the performances staged by secret societies, showed one face while open and another while closed. This example changes from an eagle to a quasi-human spirit when it is opened.

WAR AND PEACE

As was common throughout the area, Kwakwaka'wakw groups engaged in both peaceful and violent interactions. Intermarriage was common, and chiefs often tried to best their rivals through peaceful potlatches. However, villages and clans also engaged in frequent raids and small wars. Raiding parties traveled by dugout canoe, with as many as 40 or 50 men per boat. The warriors wore wooden helmets and armor made of wooden slats. For weapons, they used bows and arrows, clubs, spears, and knives.

This Kwakwaka'wakw warrior stands ready for battle, holding a wooden spear. Like other Northwest tribes, the Kwakwaka'wakw engaged in frequent small wars.

BUTTON BLANKETS

The Kwakwaka'wakw were never shy about flaunting their status, and when they received new materials from the Europeans, they used them to create new ways of displaying their power. Button blankets, popular among several Northwest tribes, were one such creation. Made from fabric and ordinary mother-of-pearl buttons, these robes functioned as wearable totem poles, indicating the rank, social status, and family history of the wearer. They were worn only on special occasions, such as feasts and potlatches.

This Kwakwaka'wakw button blanket features a stylized eagle. Most blankets stuck to the red, white, and black color scheme, since these colors had important symbolic meanings.

The Arctic and Subarctic peoples had a range of experiences after European contact. Some benefited from the fur trade, which extended into their lands from both the Northeast Woodlands and the Pacific Northwest. Many would also struggle to preserve their traditional ways of life.

Aleut winter houses were built partially underground to help insulate them from the cold. The houses were divided into family units by woven mats. The only entrance was a hole in the roof, accessed by a ladder.

HARD TIMES FOR THE ALEUTS

The Aleuts lived on a chain of islands that stretched southwest from Alaska. When Russian fur traders arrived in 1741, the hospitable Aleuts were eager to trade for European goods. Unfortunately, the trade did not go well. Russian "freebooters"—men who were not under government control—treated the people cruelly. The Aleuts fought back, but they were no match for the Russians. The islanders were also hit hard by European diseases. In 1799, the Russian government ended the slaughter, but the damage had been done. Between 1741 and 1825, the Aleut population dropped from 18,000 to 1,500. Ninety percent of the Aleuts were dead.

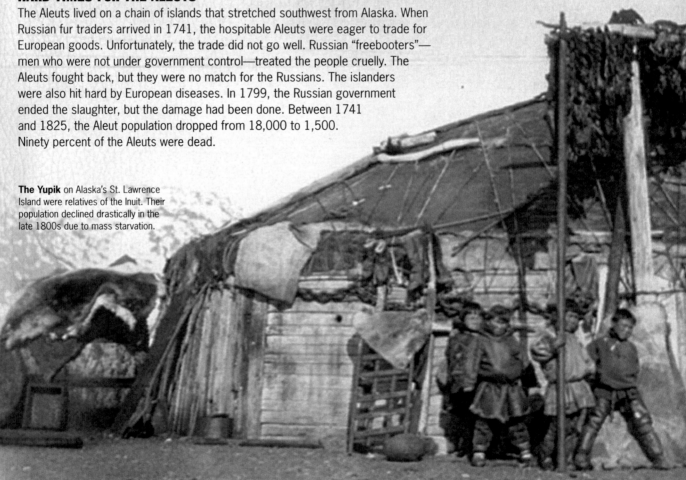

The Yupik on Alaska's St. Lawrence Island were relatives of the Inuit. Their population declined drastically in the late 1800s due to mass starvation.

INUIT PROSPERITY

In the 1700s, both Europeans and Americans encouraged the Inuit to bring furs to the trading posts they established in the North. In return, the Inuit received modern weapons such as steel harpoons and rifles, which were highly valued. As trade increased, the Inuit enjoyed a period of prosperity and artistic creativity. They made outstanding carvings of soapstone and ivory, many of which can now be viewed in museums around the world. However, the increased demand for pelts from white traders led to a sharp decline in the populations of many sea and land mammals in the area.

SOAPSTONE FIGURE

Hudson's Bay Company held a monopoly on Indian trade in a large region of eastern Canada. Here, Native people exchange furs for goods at one of the British company's many trading posts.

INUIT PROBLEMS

Before the rise of the fur trade, the Inuit in eastern Canada encountered European explorers searching for a Northwest Passage. Later, in the 1700s, they met American whaling ships in need of a place to spend the winter. These contacts were friendly, but already European diseases had been planted. The Inuit population began to decline throughout the Arctic, and by the end of the 19th century, it had dropped by roughly two-thirds. In addition, some Inuit bands traded furs for liquor. Unfamiliar with alcohol, men began to spend their summers drinking instead of storing supplies for the winter. Some villages faced the dark winters with little or no food, and many Inuit died of starvation.

ENCOUNTERS IN THE SUBARCTIC

From the 17th to the 19th centuries, the Subarctic people dealt with fur traders from England, France, Canada, and the United States. During this time, there were a few outbreaks of violence, but the two largest tribes, the Cree and the Ojibwe, fought each other more than the outsiders. The more numerous Cree, armed with guns provided by the fur companies, used force to take over the lands of the Ojibwe, who straddled the border between the Northeast and Subarctic regions. Although the fur trade brought prosperity at first, by the mid-19th century all tribes were becoming demoralized. Facing loss of land and population, most were willing to settle on reservations established by the Canadian government in the late 1800s.

An ulu was an all-purpose Inuit cooking knife. Its blade was traditionally made of polished slate, but after European contact, the Inuit began making ulus with blades of steel.

THE VIRGINIA FRONTIER

Founded in 1607, Jamestown was the first permanent English settlement in North America. As such, it provided a preview of future interactions between Europeans and Indians—an initial phase of friendship followed by violent conflict and war.

YEARS OF UNEASY PEACE

After the failure of the Roanoke Colony in the 1580s, the English continued to harbor a desire to establish a permanent colony in the New World. They finally succeeded in 1607, with the founding of Jamestown in present-day Virginia.

The Jamestown colonists survived the first few years only because the people of the Powhatan Confederacy helped them with gifts of food and showed them how to grow and gather more. The colonists, however, were often uncooperative and sometimes demanded food rather than trading for it. In 1609, Chief Wahunsonacock (known to the settlers as Powhatan) warned them: "Why will you destroy us who supply you with food? . . . We are unarmed, and willing to give you what you ask, if you come in a friendly manner. . . . Take away your guns and swords, . . . or you may die in the same manner."

For several years, the settlers'

muskets and cannons gave them an edge, even though the Powhatan Confederacy, made up of more than 20 tribes, numbered more than 14,000 people.

The English settlers at Jamestown often had to trade with the Indians for food. In this illustration, the English visit a Powhatan fort. Spread out before them is the food being offered in trade.

THE TOBACCO BOOM

Conditions changed after 1610, when John Rolfe, one of Jamestown's leaders, cultivated a new form of tobacco. Formed by crossing the local variety (which the English didn't care for) with a strain from the West Indes, Rolfe's plant was

sweet enough for the European palate, but still grew well in the Virginia soil. The new tobacco caused a sensation in England, and Jamestown now had a cash crop that was worth millions of dollars. Suddenly, the colonists were planting the precious tobacco plants wherever they could find an open patch of ground.

Soon, shipload after shipload of new English settlers began arriving in Virginia. The demand for land skyrocketed throughout the region, and that spelled disaster for the Powhatans.

THE POCAHONTAS INTERLUDE

Even before Rolfe developed his crop, the conflict between the English and the Powhatans had broken out into open warfare; the tobacco boom only made

Jamestown was the first permanent English settlement in North America. Today, a partial reconstruction of the colony stands at the site.

Chief Powhatan's cloak was given to the English in exchange for a European cloak during a friendly ceremony in 1608.

things worse. Although Powhatan losses were heavy, the Indians continued fighting until 1613, when the colonists kidnapped Pocahontas, the favorite daughter of Chief Powhatan. At this point, Powhatan immediately made peace.

While Pocahontas was being held by the English, John Rolfe fell in love with her, and the two were married in 1614. Two years later, Rolfe took his bride, now called Lady Rebecca by the English, to his home country, where she was very popular among the people. The sponsors of the Jamestown Colony pointed to Pocahontas as evidence

largest assault the English had ever seen on American soil. Of the estimated 1,200 Jamestown colonists, 347 were massacred. The Powhatans thought that such a crushing attack would convince the English to go home.

Instead, the settlers fought back. They burned villages and sold captured Powhatan women and children into slavery. They destroyed Opechancanough's main town and killed 800 Indians in a single day.

Over the next 20 years, the Powhatans lost more and more land as the land-hungry settlers moved further inland from their original settlement on the coast. In the meantime, European diseases cut further into the Native population.

THE FINAL WAR
Twenty years later, in 1644, Opechancanough, now in his eighties, launched one more attack on Jamestown. By this time, however, the Powhatans had been badly weakened by

Pocahontas and John Smith

John Smith was a leader of Jamestown. According to legend, he was captured in 1607 and taken to meet Chief Powhatan. The chief ordered his warriors to put Smith to death, but Powhatan's daughter Pocahontas threw herself on the Englishman, begging for his life. Powhatan relented and granted Smith his freedom. Although this story is popular, scholars now think Smith may have invented it—he didn't even write it down until 10 years after the incident.

designated as Indian. A few other tribes retained elements of their culture through the 1800s, but it was clear that Europeans were now the masters of the region.

"Why will you destroy us who supply you with food?"
—Chief Powhatan

that American Indians could be converted to the European way of life, and that English colonists would be safe in America. In 1617, as the couple began their return trip, Pocahontas became ill and died. She was 21 years old. The following year, her grief-stricken father died, and his half-brother Opechancanough became the dominant chief. The new chief immediately began preparing for war.

THE WAR OF 1622
Opechancanough spent months stirring his people into a frenzy. In 1622, accompanied by a large band of warriors, he launched the

measles and smallpox, and numbered only about 5,000. After two years of bitter warfare, the Powhatans were forced to surrender. Opechancanough was captured by the colonists, but refused to sign a treaty with them; the chief was eventually shot and killed by a guard.

His successor signed treaties with the English colonists in 1646 and 1647. These restricted the Powhatans to a few small areas that were later designated as reservations. By about 1720, there were 2,000 Powhatans left. Only two of the member tribes—the Pamunkey and the Accomac—still held land that was officially

C. Smith taketh the King of Pamavnkee prisoner. 1608.

Opechancanough wanted to drive the English out of Virginia. This illustration depicts an early encounter between the future chief and English explorer John Smith.

THE CONFLICT IN NEW ENGLAND

The first English colonies in New England received vital help from the Indians living in the area. The Indians brought food, and taught the colonists how to grow the local crops. Even in these peaceful times, however, the seeds of conflict were being sown.

Metacom was a proud leader of the Wampanoag people.

A PEACEFUL START

In 1620, the English Pilgrims founded Plymouth Colony in modern Massachusetts. At first, the Indians and colonists lived in peace. In 1621, the English joined members of the Wampanoag nation in a friendly feast now known as the First Thanksgiving.

THE PEQUOT WAR

As more and more colonists came to New England, they put increasing pressure on the Indians to give up land. Indian sachems were willing to put their mark on treaties, but they didn't share the Europeans' ideas about exclusive land ownership.

DIAGRAM OF THE ATTACK ON THE PEQUOT FORT

They assumed they were simply agreeing to share the land with the colonists, and were horrified when colonists told them to leave the area. When new colonial settlements were established in the Connecticut River Valley, the Pequot Indians were ready to strike back.

The Pequot War was short and bloody. In 1637, after the Pequots laid siege to Fort Saybrook at the mouth of the Connecticut River, a large colonial force, with some Indian allies, attacked a Pequot fort. The Pequots drove back the first attack, but the colonists set fire to the village, trapping hundreds of Indians, including women and children. The Pequots never recovered. Most of the survivors were sold into slavery in Bermuda.

The fortified village of the Pequot tribe was destroyed by English colonists in May 1637.

THE FINAL NEW ENGLAND WAR

By 1670, the colonists numbered more than 50,000, putting increasing land pressure on the Indians. Repeated epidemics of smallpox and other European diseases continued to weaken the Indians in the area, who now numbered only about 10,000.

The key player in the next conflict was a strong Indian leader named Metacom. Metacom was sachem of the Wampanoag and son of the great Massasoit, who had been present at the First Thanksgiving. Metacom hated what he saw happening to his people. In addition to the loss of land, he felt a growing sense of humiliation. Massachusetts officials repeatedly ordered him to come to them to answer questions, and some colonists added to his humiliation by calling him "King Philip" as a way of mocking his authority over the tribe.

For four years, Metacom worked hard to forge an alliance with about three-quarters of New England's Indian nations, including the Nipmuck, Pokanoket, Sokokis, Narragansett, and Massachusett. The allies met secretly in forest glens and set up forges to make and repair their own guns.

In June 1675, Metacom launched a series of coordinated attacks on colonial villages in the Connecticut River Valley. Over the next 10 months, the Wampanoags and their allies attacked town after town. Of the 90 colonial towns, 52 were attacked; many were burned to the ground and hundreds of colonists were killed. The colonists felt their backs were to the wall and were constantly afraid of further Indian attacks.

Metacom and his allies could not maintain their advantage, however. For nearly a year, there had been no planting or harvest, and little time for hunting and fishing. Many Indian villages were close to starvation. A colonial attack on a stronghold in Narragansett Bay, known as the Great Swamp Fight, ended in the death of some 600 Narragansetts. To make matters worse, some Indians sided with the colonial army, often serving as spies or scouts.

Mary Rowlandson

In the midst of the brutality, there were occasional touches of kindness. In February 1676, a band of Narragansett and Nipmuck Indians raided the village of Lancaster, Massachusetts, killing 35 colonists and taking 24 captives, including Mary Rowlandson. Mary spent more than 11 weeks with the Indians, until she was freed for a ransom. Her captors moved often to avoid colonial forces and they were constantly on the brink of starvation. Mary was once taken to meet Metacom, who invited her to dinner. "He gave me a pancake, about as big as two fingers . . ." she wrote later. "I thought I never tasted pleasanter meat in my life." Later, during a march, Metacom spotted her, took her hand, and said, "Two weeks more and you shall be Mistress of your home again."

Metacom suffered a severe setback when he tried to establish a camp north of Albany as a place to recover. The powerful Iroquois Confederacy drove his forces back into New England. In August, Massachusetts colonists attacked his camp and killed 173 of his followers. Metacom escaped, but his wife and nine-year-old son were captured. "My heart is broken," he told a friend. "Now I am ready to die."

On August 12, 1676, a colonial militia attacked Metacom's camp before dawn.

The Pilgrims came to America to escape religious discrimination. They advocated total separation from the Church of England.

He was shot by an Indian auxiliary. His head was cut off and later raised on a pole in the town of Plymouth. His hands were cut off and put on public display for a viewing fee.

The war against the English colonists cost the Native people of the Northeast dearly. Roughly 40 percent of the Indian population was killed or removed. Metacom's wife and son were sold into slavery along with about 500 others. Roughly 1,000 colonists died, or five percent of the total population—higher than the percentage who died during World War II. Every Indian nation in the area was reduced to ruin. In the early 1700s, a bounty of $500 was offered by the government of Massachusetts for every Indian scalp.

The friendly relations enjoyed at the "First Thanksgiving" did not last long.

THE CONFLICT MOVES WEST

Throughout the 1700s and early 1800s, American colonists moved westward, eager for land in the fertile Ohio River Valley and the Great Lakes region beyond. The Native tribes put up fierce resistance, but they had little chance of winning against the ever-increasing stream of settlers from the east.

General Anthony Wayne had risen to prominence during the American Revolution. His fiery temper earned him the nickname "Mad Anthony."

PONTIAC'S REBELLION

Pontiac was the chief of a confederation of Ottawa, Potawatomi, and Ojibwe tribes. Inspired by a spiritual leader named Neolin, he began urging his people to join him in a crusade to drive out the American settlers, abandon all European ways, and return to traditional Indian ways of life.

In 1763, Pontiac saw an opportunity to rally his forces. For years, France had been fighting Great Britain over competing territorial claims in North America, in a conflict known as the French and Indian War. After years of losing, the British had emerged victorious, forcing France to give up its huge colony of Canada. However, there was a gap of several months before a treaty could be signed. During that time, Pontiac used his outstanding speaking skills to build an alliance that included most of the tribes in the region.

Pontiac's plan was to launch surprise attacks on British forts, especially Fort Detroit, on the site of the present-day city of that name. He thought that the remaining French forces in Canada would then join his forces to drive the British out of the area. The British, however, managed to fend off Pontiac's forces at Detroit, and the siege dragged on through the summer and fall.

Meanwhile, Indian forces captured most of the other British forts. War parties attacked frontier settlements and killed hundreds of settlers. But by winter, the alliance fell apart. As long as the British held Detroit, they controlled the gateway to the middle of the continent. In addition, the fighting had given the Indians little time to harvest crops or to hunt. Soon, word came that France and England had finalized a treaty. That treaty and his people's hunger convinced Pontiac to sign a truce at last.

Pontiac used his speaking abilities to build his alliance. In this illustration, he holds a wampum belt as he meets with representatives from allied tribes.

LITTLE TURTLE'S WAR

As more settlers moved into Ohio, chiefs and warriors of several nations strove to prevent them from crossing the Ohio River. The Indians found a brilliant military leader in a Miami chief named Little Turtle.

On two occasions in the early 1790s, American armies tried to defeat Little Turtle's coalition. On both occasions, the clever Miami chief used trickery to avoid defeat and inflict heavy casualties. More than 600 Americans were killed—the biggest U.S. loss in any of the Indian wars.

In 1794, General "Mad Anthony" Wayne, under orders from President George Washington, was sent to lead another force against the Indian coalition. Little Turtle knew he could not defeat Wayne, so he urged his fellow leaders to seek peace. They refused, and the Indians took the field against Wayne at the Battle of Fallen Timbers in August 1795. The Americans won decisively, and the Indians eventually gave up millions of acres of land.

TECUMSEH

The land between the Ohio River and the Great Lakes, known as the Old Northwest, was considered untapped wilderness by the land-hungry American settlers. But to the Indian peoples, this land was home—and they did not want to give it up.

In the early 19th century, a Shawnee war chief and orator named Tecumseh emerged as one of the greatest Indian leaders. He began urging the creation of an independent Indian nation, one made of allied tribes stretching down the middle of the continent from the Great Lakes to the Gulf of Mexico. He traveled great distances during this time, using his speaking skills to add to his alliance.

The Battle of the Thames was a decisive American victory in the War of 1812. This illustration shows Tecumseh being killed by Colonel Richard M. Johnson of Kentucky, though it is not certain that Johnson actually fired the fatal shot.

In 1808, Tecumseh and his brother Tenskwatawa, known as the Prophet, founded a town in Indiana called Tippecanoe, which as also known as Prophetstown. Three years later, while Tecumseh was away urging Creeks and Chickasaws to join his alliance, the Prophet made the mistake of attacking a militia force commanded by William Henry Harrison, governor of Indiana. Harrison struck back vigorously, overran the Indian warriors, and burned Prophetstown to the ground. After the destruction of Prophetstown, the Prophet disappeared into obscurity and Tecumseh was left with no home base and a group of badly shaken followers. He now knew that, even if they were unified, his people could never defeat the armies of the United States.

Soon afterward, the United States declared war against Great Britain in what became known as the War of 1812. Seeing an opportunity, Tecumseh went to Canada to join forces with the British. As a brigadier general in the British army, he organized a strong force of Indians and British. The combined army fought well, but Tecumseh was killed on October 5, 1813, at the Battle of the Thames. His coalition quickly disbanded.

BLACK HAWK'S WAR

By 1830, white Americans assumed that all of the Old Northwest was free of Indian war parties. They moved into lands in present-day Illinois without worrying about Native resistance. The leaders of the Sauk and Fox tribes, who originally inhabited the area, were split over how to respond to the movements of the settlers. One chief, Keokuk, decided to accept the expansion, but a chief named Black Hawk refused. Black Hawk was a respected war chief who had fought in the War of 1812, but he was now over 60 years old. What became known as

Black Hawk's War was a feeble effort on the part of the aging warrior to build one more coalition. Only a few Winnebagos joined his Sauks. In an 1832 battle, U.S. forces launched a vicious attack on Black Hawk's band. Trapped in a swamp near the Mississippi River, the Indians asked for a truce. The request was ignored and the army killed far more people than was necessary.

Black Hawk surrendered and was taken on a tour of eastern cities, where he was presented to the public as a spectacle. That was the end of Indian resistance in the Old Northwest.

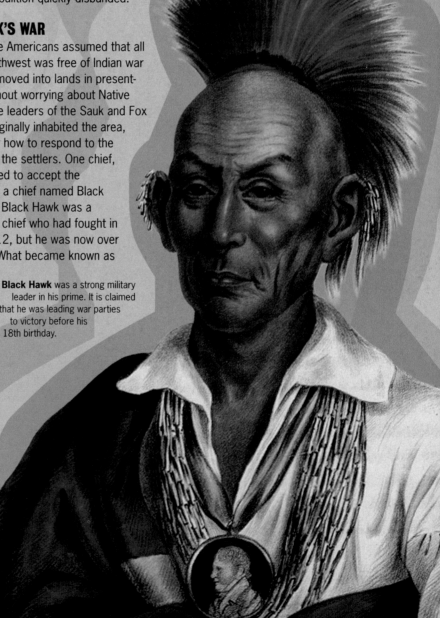

Black Hawk was a strong military leader in his prime. It is claimed that he was leading war parties to victory before his 18th birthday.

American Independence

In 1776, the American colonies declared independence from England, and the United States became its own nation. Unfortunately, although the new country's Declaration of Independence stated that all men were created equal, the Indians would get no better treatment at the hands of the new government than the old.

OTHER INDIAN STRUGGLES TO SURVIVE

The story of the European conquest is in many ways the story of westward expansion, as white settlements extended gradually from the east. However, this leaves out many Indian struggles that occurred at other times and places, but which still involved valiant efforts to maintain traditional ways of life.

THE BIRTH OF THE SEMINOLES

After establishing the colony of St. Augustine on the Florida coast in 1565, the Spanish began establishing missions throughout the Southeast. For a time, they controlled much of the area. In 1669, however, the English established colonies in the Carolinas and began enlisting Indian warriors to help them conquer Spanish territory in Florida—one of many cases in which Indian societies were caught up in the rivalries of European nations. Creeks and Yuchis invaded Florida, destroyed Spanish missions, and killed or enslaved thousands of Christian Indians. By 1750, many of Florida's original Timucua, Apalachee, and Calusa Indians had become slaves on colonial plantations; many others had been sold in the West Indies.

The combination of disease and warfare wore down the Southeastern Indians. Several tribes simply disappeared between 1650 and 1750. Members of a number of tribes, including Hitchitis, Yamasees, Lower Creeks, and Yuchis, established camps in deserted areas of Florida. They were joined in time by many escaped African slaves. This group became known as the *Isty-Semole,* a Creek phrase meaning something like "wild men," which actually indicated that they lived by hunting. By the late 1700s, they became known as Seminoles.

THE FALL OF THE IROQUOIS

Before the American Revolution, the Iroquois Confederacy held a strong position in the Northeast, due in part to a history of alliances with European powers. When the American colonies declared their independence from Great Britain in 1776, the Iroquois had to decide which side to support. A Mohawk chief named Joseph Brant urged the confederacy to side with the British. Brant was supported by Sir William Johnson, the British superintendent of Indian affairs, who had been adopted into the Mohawk nation and lived among the Indians. After his death in 1774, Johnson was replaced by his son, Guy, who continued to support Brant and his allies.

Brant had become known as "the monster" for leading vicious raids against American colonists who had started pioneer farms in the Iroquois territory west of the Hudson River. When the American Revolution began, Guy Johnson took Brant to England, where the Mohawk chief was treated as a celebrity by the public and made an officer in the British army.

This 1769 document confirms that the Iroquois received payment for lands ceded to the British under a treaty. The signatures of the Iroquois are accompanied by their totem symbols.

The Castillo de San Marcos was built in St. Augustine by the Spanish in the 17th century to defend the city against attacks.

When Brant returned home, he persuaded the Mohawks, Onondagas, Cayugas, and Senecas to fight alongside the British. However, the other two Iroquois nations—the Oneida and the Tuscarora—sided with the American colonists.

The division of the Iroquois Confederacy was devastating for both sides. Over the course of the American Revolution, the two factions attacked each other's villages ruthlessly, and the people became disheartened and demoralized. Brant was also held responsible for the massacre of American settlers at Cherry Valley, New York, and Wyoming, Pennsylvania.

In 1779, General George Washington sent an army of 4,000 troops on a march of destruction through southern New York in retaliation for the massacres. The Americans burned Iroquois villages, and destroyed their homes, crops, and livestock, further devastating the people of the six nations.

When the war ended, Brant and his pro-English followers crossed into Canada, where they established new homes in lands controlled by the British. The rest of the Iroquois, under two new leaders—Red Jacket and Cornplanter—formed peaceful relations with the United States. However, the Iroquois had lost their position of power in the region. Over the next 50 years, most of the surviving bands moved onto reservations.

THE PUEBLO REVOLT

In the late 17th century, the government established under Juan de Oñate (see pp.80–81) continued to exert control over the Southwest. The Native people were forced to work the farms at the Spanish missions, and many had been converted to Christianity by the priests. However, when the Spanish weren't looking, most of the Indians continued to follow their traditional customs.

During this time, Popé, a Pueblo shaman, began leading secret meetings to unify his people's opposition to the Spanish. In 1680, he orchestrated a successful revolt.

The Pueblo Revolt was one of the most successful instances of Indian resistance to European authority. Because of the efforts of Popé and his followers, some Pueblo villages remained free of Spanish control for 150 years.

Rising up against their rulers, the Pueblos killed more than 400 Spaniards, and forced the rest to flee. After more than 80 years of brutality and oppression, the Pueblo people were finally free from Spanish rule.

Joseph Brant, also known as Thayendanegea, was educated at an English school in Connecticut. When he visited England from 1775 to 1776, he had his portrait made by the court painter George Romney.

Some Pueblo tribes held onto their independence for another 150 years.

With the Spanish gone, Popé became the new ruler of his people, but not everyone agreed with his decisions. When he died in 1688, there was a series of power struggles among the Pueblo villages. Four years later, the Spanish took advantage of the lack of unity among the Pueblos to complete a successful reconquest of the region.

This time, the Spanish rule was less extensive than before. Efforts to eradicate traditional Pueblo culture were less extreme, and some villages were never reconquered. Although most Pueblo people once again lived under European authority, the Hopi and a few other tribes held onto their independence for another 150 years.

LAST CONFLICTS IN THE EAST

Although many tribes fought fiercely to defend their traditional ways of life, others thought they might survive by adopting the ways of white Americans. This strategy was followed most notably by the Southeast nations known as the "Five Civilized Tribes." The effort was launched with the support of many white Americans, but this support was soon outweighed by the desire for Indian land.

"CIVILIZING" INDIAN LIFE

The term *Five Civilized Tribes* was applied to the Cherokee, Chickasaw, Choctaw, Creek, and Seminole nations. Their campaign to adopt white Americans' ways of living began in the mid- to late 1700s. During this time, the tribes established European-style farms, with fields of corn, wheat, and other crops; they also started orchards and raised livestock, practices that were unknown prior to European contact. Longhouses were replaced by log cabins or frame houses. The Native societies built schools and churches, and invited missionaries to teach their children and to convert those who were willing to become Christians.

THE CHEROKEE MODEL

The Cherokee, the largest of the five tribes, became a model of the effort to assimilate. By the 1820s, they had built prosperous villages and developed a system of government with a constitution based on that of the United States. They owned grist mills, saw mills, hundreds of spinning wheels and looms, and more than 20,000 head of cattle. Under the leadership of John Ross, their principal chief, the Cherokee hoped to establish themselves as a sovereign nation, located within the United States but not subject to its government or laws.

In addition, a Cherokee named Sequoyah invented an entire written language for his people. As was the case with other North American languages, Cherokee had previously existed only as a spoken language—writing had been unknown before the arrival of the Europeans. Like many of his people, Sequoyah came into frequent contact with white settlers, who used writing for a variety of purposes. He became fascinated by their "talking leaves" and decided to invent a system of writing for the Cherokee language. After working on the project for 12 years, he introduced the Cherokee alphabet to his people in 1821. Although tribal elders were initially skeptical, Seqoyah's alphabet eventually caught on. In 1828, the nation began publishing a newspaper called the *Cherokee Phoenix*, the first American Indian newspaper in history.

ENTER ANDREW JACKSON

Despite the heroic efforts of the five tribes, none could hold back the ever-larger waves of white settlers demanding land. Without opposition from the state governments, settlers simply stampeded onto Indian territory.

Seminole villages in the 1800s displayed a range of cultural influences. Although the villagers here carry guns and raise livestock, the huts are similar to those used by Florida's original first people.

In 1813, a group of Creeks, responding to the oratory of Tecumseh (see p.22), overran a fort in Alabama, killing nearly 400 whites and pro-white Indians. The federal government responded by sending General Andrew Jackson to Alabama at the head of an army that included pro-white Creeks and Cherokees. At the Battle of Horseshoe Bend, Jackson won a smashing victory. Many Creeks fled to Florida where they joined the Seminole; two-thirds of the Creek lands were ceded, making up large areas of Georgia and Alabama.

In 1817, Jackson marched into Florida, which at the time was still a colony of Spain. During the ensuing conflict, Jackson and his army laid waste to many Indian towns. In the end, the Seminoles were forced to allow settlers onto some areas of Florida land.

The Cotton Gin

In 1792, Eli Whitney, a college student from Connecticut, was visiting a Southern plantation, when he heard some men discussing why cotton could not be grown for a profit. The problem was that it took too long for a worker to pull the sticky seeds from the fibers that were used to make cloth. Within two weeks, Whitney had developed a device called a cotton gin (short for *engine*), which removed the seeds by pulling the cotton through a screen. With Whitney's invention, one man could clean as much cotton in an hour as 11 men could accomplish by hand.

Overnight, cotton became a highly profitable crop. Plantation owners throughout the South planted more and more cotton. These owners were soon joined by hundreds of newcomers, who spread cotton all along the Gulf Coast. As more plantations were established, the population of the region soared. Unfortunately, the rise of the cotton industry also led to a huge increase in the demand for Indian lands. Now more than ever, white Americans were eager to drive the Southeastern Indians out of their traditional homes.

Indian removal has been called one of the blackest chapters in American history.

Conflict between Indians and settlers continued through the 1820s. Georgia, Alabama, and Mississippi all passed laws that outlawed tribal governments and placed the Indians under direct control of the states, whose policies were generally far less favorable to Native people than those of the national government.

THE INDIAN REMOVAL ACT

In spite of pleas by the Five Civilized Tribes and many white supporters, the U.S. Government did nothing to help. Instead, Andrew Jackson, who had been elected president two years earlier, signed a law known as the Indian Removal Act of 1830. The new law gave the government the power to force Indians east of the Mississippi to relocate to areas farther west. What resulted was a period that leading historian Alvin M. Josephy later called "one of the blackest chapters in American history."

Andrew Jackson was a complex figure. As president, his liberal political ideals were seemingly contradicted by his policies toward American Indians.

The Seminole were brave fighters, but were no match for the forces of the United States. This 1843 watercolor depicts a Seminole chief named Tuko-See-Mathla.

WRITE IT IN CHEROKEE

In Sequoyah's Cherokee alphabet, each letter represents a syllable, such as "mi" or "mo." On the opposite page are some Cherokee words, which you can try writing for yourself. Keep in mind that even though some Cherokee letters look like English letters, the sounds they make are usually very different.

Cherokee letter					
D a *(Pronunciation)*	R e	T i	Ꭿ o	Ꮕ u	i v
Ꮧ ga Ꭷ ka	Ꭶ ge	Ꭹ gi	A go	J gu	E gv
Ꭺ ha	Ꭾ he	Ꭿ hi	Ꮄ ho	Ꮀ hu	Ꮟ hv
W la	Ꮈ le	Ꮅ li	Ꮏ lo	M lu	Ꮑ lv
Ꮂ ma	Ꮊ me	H mi	Ꮔ mo	Ꭼ mu	
Ꮎ na Ꮏ hna Ꮐ nah	Ꮄ ne	Ꮒ ni	Z no	Ꮔ nu	Ꮕ nv
Ꮖ qua	Ꮄ que	Ꮗ qui	Ꮖ quo	Ꮙ quu	Ꮛ quv
Ꮜ sa Ꮝ s	Ꮞ se	Ꮜ si	Ꮠ so	Ꮡ su	R sv
Ꮄ da Ꮣ ta	Ꮥ de Ꮦ te	Ꮧ di Ꮨ ti	V do	S du	Ꮫ dv
Ꮬ dla Ꮭ tla	L tle	C tli	Ꮯ tlo	Ꮰ tlu	Ꮱ tlv
Ꮳ tsa	Ꮴ tse	Ꮵ tsi	K tso	J tsu	Ꮷ tsv
Ꮹ wa	Ꮺ we	Ꮻ wi	Ꮼ wo	Ꮽ wu	Ꮾ wv
Ꮿ ya	Ᏸ ye	Ᏹ yi	Ᏺ yo	Ᏻ yu	B yv

WOLF

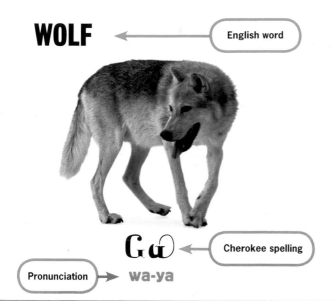

English word

Cherokee spelling

Pronunciation

Ꮐꮹ

wa-ya

BASKET

ᏔᎷᏥ

ta-lu-tsi

DOG

ᎩᏟ

gi-tli

BEAR

ᏲᏅ

yo-nv

EAGLE

ᏩᎭᎵ

wo-ha-li

HORSE

ᏐᏈᎵ

so-qui-li

FISH

ᎠᏣᏗ

a-tsa-di

BREAD

ᎦᏚ

ga-du

PIE

ᎨᎵᏍᎩ

ge-li-s-gi

BUFFALO

ᏲᎾᏍᏏ

yo-na-s-si

RATTLESNAKE

ᎤᏦᎾᏘ

u-tso-na-ti

THE TRAIL WHERE THEY CRIED

When the Indian Removal policy was instituted, the Five Civilized Tribes were the first to be affected. The journey west was so difficult that the Cherokee called it *nuna-daa-ut-sun'y,* meaning "the trail where they cried." The term was later shortened to "Trail of Tears."

THE REMOVALS BEGIN

Under the Indian Removal Act, tribes in the east were forced by the government to move to areas in the west, where their people had no history and no connection to the land. Officially, tribes had to agree to these moves by signing treaties, but in practice this didn't make much difference. Tribes were often coerced into signing treaties, and the Native people who signed them weren't always legitimate representatives of the people of the tribe.

The first relocations began in 1831, when around 4,000 Choctaws made the

The Trail of Tears was a horrific experience for the Cherokee. Nearly 8,000 of the travelers died.

journey to western Arkansas. The people suffered badly along the way, largely because government agents kept much of the money intended for food and other supplies. Some of the agents hired rotten boats for river crossings, caring little if they sank—in their eyes, it would simply mean fewer Indians to worry about.

The Chickasaws were next and made the move peacefully. The Creeks, however, became bitterly divided. One group helped the army put down the "uprising" of the group that refused to be removed. Once peace was established, all the Creeks were ordered to move to Arkansas. A cold winter increased their suffering on the trail.

"We were drove off like wolves," one Creek reported later, "and our people's feet were bleeding with long marches."

SEMINOLE RESISTANCE

When the Seminole people were told to prepare for the move to Indian Territory in present-day Oklahoma, they refused. Many moved deeper into the Florida Everglades. Throughout the 1830s, they fought the U.S. Army to a standstill. The fighting, while sporadic, was vicious, and there was heavy loss of life. Under their brilliant leader, Osceola, the Seminole attacked isolated army units and often wiped them out entirely.

After several years of conflict and the deaths of 1,500 soldiers, the United States

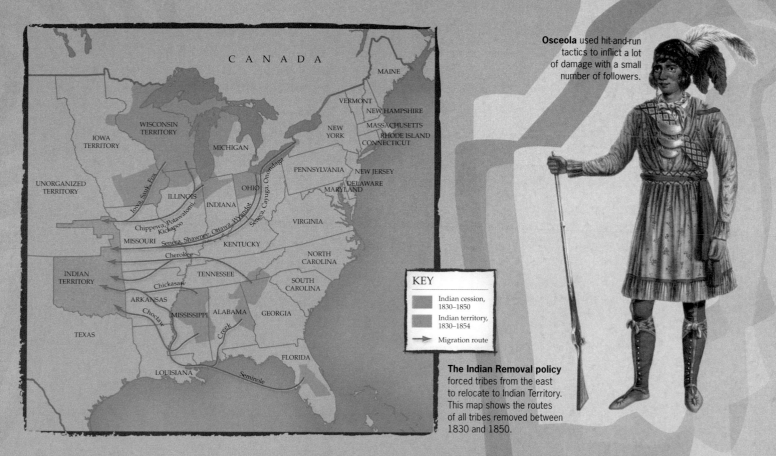

CANADA

MAINE

VERMONT
NEW HAMPSHIRE
MASSACHUSETTS
RHODE ISLAND
CONNECTICUT

NEW YORK

WISCONSIN TERRITORY

MICHIGAN

IOWA TERRITORY

PENNSYLVANIA
NEW JERSEY
DELAWARE
MARYLAND

UNORGANIZED TERRITORY

Iowa Sauk-Fox

ILLINOIS
INDIANA
OHIO

Seneca, Cayuga, Onondaga

VIRGINIA

Chippewa, Potawatomi Kickapoo

MISSOURI
Seneca, Shawnee, Ottawa, Wyandot

KENTUCKY

Cherokee

NORTH CAROLINA

INDIAN TERRITORY

TENNESSEE

SOUTH CAROLINA

Chickasaw

ARKANSAS

Choctaw

MISSISSIPPI
ALABAMA
GEORGIA

Creek

TEXAS

LOUISIANA

FLORIDA

Seminole

KEY
▇ Indian cession, 1830–1850
▇ Indian territory, 1830–1854
→ Migration route

Osceola used hit-and-run tactics to inflict a lot of damage with a small number of followers.

The Indian Removal policy forced tribes from the east to relocate to Indian Territory. This map shows the routes of all tribes removed between 1830 and 1850.

finally invited Osceola to a peace talk. It was a trap. Osceola was taken prisoner and moved to Fort Moultrie in the bay of Charleston, South Carolina. He died of malaria a few months later.

At this point, most of the Seminole submitted to removal. However, several hundred remained deep in the Everglades and the army could not dislodge them. Their descendants remain there today.

THE MARCH OF THE CHEROKEE

In the early 1830s, the state of Georgia attempted to force the Cherokee off their land, independent of the federal government. John Ross and his people fought the action by going to the courts. Their hopes soared when the Supreme Court ruled in favor of the Cherokee, declaring that only the federal

Nearly 8,000 Cherokee died during the journey.

government could make decisions involving Indian tribes. However, the victory was short-lived, since President Jackson and Congress continued to push for the Cherokee to be removed.

In 1838, General Winfield Scott was ordered to enforce the relocation of the Cherokee. First, he had stockades built to act as holding pens Then, as one of the soldiers reported, "Families at dinner were startled by the sudden gleam of bayonets in the doorway and rose up to be driven with blows and oaths along the weary miles that led to the stockade." Eventually, 18,000 men, women, and children were taken from their homes.

The removals continued through 1839. The journey for each group took about six months and nearly 8,000 Cherokees died along the way, of disease, exposure, and starvation. One of those who died was John Ross's wife Quatie, who had given her blanket to a cold, sick child.

A white traveler who came upon one group wrote: "We learned from the inhabitants on the road where the Indians passed, that they buried fourteen or fifteen at every stopping place, and they make a journey of ten miles per day only on average."

THE FINAL TALLY

In the end, between 80,000 and 100,000 Native people were forced to move during the period of Indian Removal. Roughly one-third died during or shortly after the journey, and once they reached their destination, the tribes were forced to live on reservations, where they were monitored by government agents. Over the coming decades, American Indians would be put through many more such devastating experiences, as the U.S. government turned increasingly toward a more systematic subjugation of Indian tribes.

THE IMPACT OF NEW DEVELOPMENTS

The 19th century was a time of extraordinary growth for the United States, which put enormous pressure on Indian societies. By 1850, almost all Indians had been pushed west of the Mississippi. Even in their new homes, however, these Native cultures were not safe from the new developments that were changing the face of the continent.

EXPANDING BORDERS

Over the course of the century, the United States acquired large areas of land, and many tribes did not fare well under the new government. In 1848, Mexico ceded a huge portion of the Southwest to the United States. as a result of losing a war. In California, the end of Mexican rule was devastating for the Indians who had lived in the missions. With no jobs and no villages to return to, they wandered aimlessly through the interior. Some turned to robbery, and others were shot by miners during the Gold Rush. It is estimated that 70,000 California Indians died between 1847 and 1859.

The first transcontinental railroad in the United States was completed at a special ceremony at Promontory Point, Utah, where a golden railroad spike was driven into the tracks.

OREGON COUNTRY 1846

RED RIVER BASIN 1816

LOUISIANA PURCHASE FROM FRANCE 1803

UNITED STATES AFTER AMERICAN REVOLUTION 1783

ORIGINAL THIRTEEN COLONIES 17TH AND 18TH CENTURIES

MEXICAN CESSION AFTER MEXICAN WAR 1848

GADSDEN PURCHASE FROM MEXICO 1853

TEXAS ANNEXATION FROM MEXICO 1845

FLORIDA ACQUISITION FROM SPAIN 1819

ALASKA PURCHASE FROM RUSSIA 1867

The United States expanded its territory greatly during the 1800s. This map shows the stages of this expansion. Each block of new territory is marked with the date of acquisition, and a description of how the land was acquired.

THE GOLD RUSH

In 1848, gold was discovered at Sutter's Mill in northern California, touching off a gold rush that lasted through the 1850s. As gold seekers arrived over land and by sea, California's non-Indian population rose from 20,000 to 100,000 in 1849; by 1852, it had become a state with 225,000 people.

The California Gold Rush was followed by several more rushes in other parts of the country. From the 1850s to the 1870s, mining towns with names such as "Dead Man's Gulch" and "Blind Man's Revenge" cropped up everywhere from Arizona to Colorado to the Dakotas.

Thousands headed for these towns, searching for gold, silver, and other precious metals. The miners paid little attention to the rights or property of the Native tribes, and violent outbreaks between whites and Indians were common. Some Indians worked in the mining camps, but conditions there were rough and degrading. Then, in 1874, gold was discovered in the Black Hills of the Dakotas. The Black Hills were the holiest lands in Sioux territory. The resulting invasion of miners led the Sioux to join with other tribes in some of the fiercest warfare of the century.

THE TRANSCONTINENTAL RAILROAD

Of all the developments in 19th-century America, none was more influential than the completion of the transcontinental railroad.

In 1869, the meeting of the Central Pacific and Union Pacific Lines at Promontory Point, Utah, sparked a transportation revolution. Until then, pioneers crossing the continent in wagon trains took four to six months to travel from Independence, Missouri, to the coast. By railroad, the journey took about a week. In addition, passengers on a train rarely faced the hazards of burning deserts or fierce storms. Nor were trains in danger of Indian attack. (Actually, tribal warriors rarely attacked wagon trains, either.)

By 1890 four more transcontinental railroad lines were in place, and the nation was crisscrossed by a total of 165,000 miles (265,485 km) of railroad. On the vast expanse of the Great Plains, towns grew along the rail lines, further reducing the land available to the Indians. Although the Plains tribes had maintained their freedom for longer than those in many areas, they too were now forced to fight for their way of life.

THE END OF THE BISON HERDS

In 1800, an estimated 30 million bison roamed the Plains. When the railroads were constructed, the Plains tribes found that the tracks cut across their hunting routes as well as the migration paths of the animals they depended on to survive.

In addition, the railroad companies hired professional hunters to kill bison. The companies used the animals to provide meat for their armies of workers and sold the hides to tanning companies in the East. William "Buffalo Bill" Cody, the most famous of these hunters, killed more than 4,000 bison in 18 months.

Some railroads even invited passengers to shoot bison as the herds ran alongside the trains. Bison possess a strange instinct to cross in front of any moving object, so trains and herds were often next to each other for miles, as the animals attempted to cross the tracks. This was far different than the responsible hunting practiced by the Indians. One observer wrote: "All over the plains, lying in disgusting masses of putrefaction along valley and hill, are strewn immense carcasses of wantonly slain buffalo. They line the Kansas Pacific Railroad for 200 miles."

At the peak of the slaughter, a million bison were killed every year. By the 1890s their numbers had been reduced from 30 million to less than 10,000. For the Plains Indians who relied on the animals, the outlook for the future was bleak.

The **California Gold Rush** brought thousands of settlers to the area in a short amount of time. Here, a prospector pans for gold in a river near a mining camp.

Buffalo Bill would later open a Wild West show that presented an idealized version of the West.

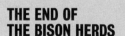

INDIAN LOSSES IN THE SOUTHWEST

In many parts of the Southwest, the pressure from the great rush of settlers led many Indian tribes to wage war on the newcomers. The fighting began on the Texas frontier in the 1840s and continued almost to the turn of the century. During this time, Native leaders such as Quanah Parker and Geronimo fought heroically to retain control of Indian lands.

WAR ON THE TEXAS FRONTIER

Many of the Texas settlers had fought the Creeks and Cherokees in the Southeast. When they moved west, they continued to regard all Indians as enemies to be pushed out of the way or killed. They virtually wiped out several small tribes.

On the northern and western borders of Texas, however, they encountered much tougher fighters—the Comanches, the Kiowas, and several bands of Apaches. The Indians fought almost continuous warfare, using hit-and-run tactics, from the 1840s into the 1870s.

One of the most successful Indian leaders was Quanah Parker, the son of a Comanche chief. Under the leadership of Parker and others, the Indians kept the U.S. Army at bay for many years. Then, in 1867, war weariness and the deaths of two valued leaders led the Comanches and Kiowas to agree to move to Indian

Covered wagons carrying settlers were a common sight in the 1800s. To Indians, they were not a welcome one.

Territory, in present-day Oklahoma. However, in the early 1870s, Parker persuaded the other chiefs to renew the fighting.

Sporadic fighting spread across five states until the army finally wore down the tribes and established peace. In 1876, Parker surrendered along with his people at the Kiowa Agency in Indian Territory. The Indians were now all but eliminated from Texas, and the Indian struggle shifted west.

THE NAVAJO LONG WALK

Like so many other Native nations, the Navajo found their lands in danger from the constant invasion of settlers. They fought back by raiding settlements and attacking groups of traveling pioneers.

In 1863, the government sent Colonel Christopher "Kit" Carson to take control. With a group of volunteer soldiers, Carson defeated one Navajo band after another. That winter, he trapped them in Canyon de Chelly, took their flocks and herds, and convinced most of them to surrender.

The Navajo were then forced to undergo what they called the "Long Walk"—a 300-mile (480 km) march to a barren stretch of land called Bosque Redondo, located just

outside an army fort in southeast New Mexico. Several hundred died on the trail.

At Bosque Redondo, the Navajo struggled for four years, trying to farm on poor soil. They were not supplied with enough food, shelter, or clothing, and around 2,000 died during this time.

Nearing the end of his life, Kit Carson realized that Bosque Redondo had been a mistake, and he persuaded government

Kit Carson was a symbol of the American West, even in his own time—a successful trapper, soldier, and frontiersman. Although he led campaigns against the Indians, he was also known for dealing fairly with them, giving him a mixed reputation among Native people.

Bosque Redondo was a completely inadequate home for the Navajo. During their stay there, they suffered from starvation, malnutrition, overcrowding, and disease.

officials to end the captivity. In 1868, a treaty was signed, allowing the Navajo to return to their homeland, which was now designated as a reservation.

Starting over was not easy. The Navajo had few sheep or horses. Their homes and orchards had been destroyed. Poverty and hardship would persist for many years.

THE LONG APACHE STRUGGLE

The Apache struggle against the Spanish, the Mexicans, and finally the white Americans seemed to go on forever. The conflict was not only long-lasting, but vicious. After years of fighting Spanish slave catchers who sold their people into slavery, the Apache at first welcomed the Americans. But it wasn't long before violence erupted; open warfare began in 1862 and continued into the 1880s.

Geronimo evaded capture for more than 25 years.

Dramatic leaders soon emerged to organize Indian forces. One, a huge man named Mangas Colorados, led the Mimbreno Apaches, and a second, Cochise, spread terror through large areas of Arizona and New Mexico by raiding white settlements with his band of Chiricahuas. These two oversaw the defense of Indian lands for nine years, until Mangas Colorados was lured out of hiding and killed. Then, a 3,000-man white volunteer force from California, with support from several Indian bands, finally forced the Apaches to make peace.

The Apaches were placed on a reservation, but hostile acts by corrupt officials led to renewed fighting. Most Apaches were tired of warfare, but a new leader named Geronimo continued to conduct raids from mountain strongholds.

Over a period of 10 years, Geronimo surrendered several times, only to escape and fight again. Over the summer of 1886, his followers became hungry and ragged. They had forced the Army to commit 5,000 soldiers to the manhunt, along with about 500 scouts. In September, Geronimo surrendered for the final time.

Geronimo and his followers were sent to a series of prisons. Although some of the prisoners were eventually allowed to return to their homeland, Geronimo was not. He later made his peace with the white world, and began making public appearances and selling autographed photos of himself. For white Americans, he was a symbol of their victory over the Indian tribes.

Geronimo successfully evaded capture by U.S. forces for more than 25 years. His Apache name was Goyathlay, meaning "one who yawns."

THE WAR FOR THE GREAT PLAINS

The struggle for control of the Great Plains was not a traditional war, with major battles leading to a final surrender. Instead, many small battles were fought throughout the West, based on local issues and disagreements. In the end, however, the result was the same: Tribe by tribe, the Indians were forced to move to reservations, while their homelands were overtaken by their conquerers.

BATTLES OVER THE TRAILS

Starting in the 1840s, the number of wagon trains crossing the Great Plains increased rapidly. Realizing that their homelands were being threatened, the Sioux, Cheyenne, Arapaho, and other tribes occasionally launched raids on these bands of settlers. When the U.S. Army was called in to retaliate, the Indians often kept the troops at bay using hit-and-run tactics.

Both sides made bold attempts to establish peace. In September 1851, the government called for a major peace conference at Fort Laramie in Colorado. An enormous throng of 10,000 Indians camped in the area around the fort, eager to establish a lasting peace. After lengthy negotiations, a treaty was signed.

Within months, the violence started again. The Indians were desperate for bison or other game and they constantly roamed outside the narrow hunting grounds assigned to them. In addition, an improved steel plow now made it possible to farm on the thick prairie sod. With the government offering 160 acres to families who would settle on the land, homesteaders were arriving by the thousands. The fact that cowboys were driving herds of cattle over their hunting trails only added to the feeling that there was no room left for the Indians.

The Great Sioux Uprising was a response by the Santee Sioux to the conditions imposed upon them by the government. Here, a band of Santee attack the settlement of New Ulm, in Minnesota.

Wagon trains were a potent symbol of the white settlers' invasion of the Plains Indian territory. Although most Indians left them alone, some tribes occasionally staged attacks on the trains, leading to retaliation by both the settlers and the army.

DOMINION OF CANADA

Seattle 1865
Spokane Plain 1858
Walla Walla 1855
Cascades 1856
Steptoe Butte 1858
Bear Paw Mountains 1877
Clearwater 1877
Yellowstone 1873
Stony Lake 1863
Big Mound 1863
Birch Creek 1878
Big Hole 1877
Whitestone Hill 1863
Grave Creek 1855
Whitebird Creek 1877
Little Bighorn 1876
Wood Lake 1862
Big Meadows 1856
Rogue River 1851
Dwyhee Forks 1866
Fetterman's Defeat 1868
Powder River 1876
Arikara 1823
Acton 1862
Steen Mountains 1878
New Ulm 1862
Pit River 1867
Platte Bridge 1865
Wounded Knee 1890
Pyramid Lake 1860
Bear River 1863
Grattan's Defeat 1854
Truckee 1860
Rush Creek 1865
Fort Kearney 1867
Meeker Agency 1879
Fort Sedgwick 1865
Massacre Canyon 1873
Sand Creek 1864
UNITED STATES OF AMERICA
Canyon de Chelly 1864
Crooked Creek 1859
Adobe Walls 1864, 1874
Washita 1868
Chustenahlah 1861
Bird Creek 1861
Skull Cave 1872
Palo Duro Canyon 1874
Soldier Spring 1868
McClellan Creek 1872
Wichita Village 1858
MEXICO
Dove Creek 1865

KEY
— Indian Reservations in 1875
✾ Battles for the West, 1850-90

Battles between whites and Indians were common in the second half of the 19th century. This map shows important battle sites, and the reservations where Indians were forced to move.

THE GREAT SIOUX UPRISING OF 1862

Frustration sometimes led Indians to attempt to engage in full-scale warfare against the settlers. One such attempt was made in 1862 by the Santee Sioux. Prior to this, the tribe had been living on a reservation. However, in the early 1860s, corruption and the government's preoccupation with the Civil War caused a breakdown in the delivery of food and supplies.

Helen Hunt Jackson

A small but growing number of white Americans were increasingly upset by what was happening to the Plains tribes. Many were influenced by the writings of Helen Hunt Jackson. In 1881, she published *Century of Dishonor,* **which chronicled the injustices committed against Indians, and called for a change in government policy. Unfortunately, the government was largely unmoved by her pleas.**

Faced with starvation and the refusal of the government to help, the Santee revolted in what became known as the Great Sioux Uprising of 1862. Led by Chief Little Crow, the Santee struck in the early morning, killing several hundred settlers on nearby farms.

After three days of raids, army reinforcements arrived and the Santees retreated westward. "Destroy everything they own," a colonel told his troops, "and drive them out into the Plains. . . . They are to be treated as maniacs or wild beasts."

By the time the army had pushed them onto the Plains, the Santee Sioux had killed around 700 settlers and 100 soldiers. A mass execution of captured Indians was ordered. President Abraham Lincoln reduced the number of captives condemned to death, but the 38 Indians who were hanged on a single scaffold still represented the largest mass hanging in U.S. history. An army force pursued the Santees who had fled onto the Plains, and killed about 500 of them. Some of the survivors joined other Sioux tribes.

THE SAND CREEK MASSACRE

The Southern Cheyenne had lived peacefully near Denver, Colorado, for years, even as the population of settlers soared to more than 50,000. These good relations were interrupted in 1864 by the Sand Creek Massacre, one of the most violent episodes in the long Indian struggle for survival.

Early that year, John Chivington, an officer in the Colorado militia, reported that Cheyennes had stolen 175 head of cattle. After Chivington launched attacks of retaliation, the governor of Colorado persuaded the Cheyenne to move peacefully to Sand Creek. No evidence was ever found that the theft had even taken place.

After the move to Sand Creek, Chivington raised a force of up to 1,000 volunteers and launched a surprise attack on the Cheyenne settlement. When some objected that the Cheyennes were living there peacefully, Chivington fumed, "I have come to kill Indians, and believe that it is right and honorable to use any means under God's heaven to kill Indians."

The Cheyennes, caught completely by surprise, were helpless as Chivington's troops rode through the camp, shooting women and children as well as men. White Antelope, a chief, stood in front of his lodge, chanting a death song, as the killing raged around him. "Nothing lives long," he sang, "except the earth and the mountains." He was shot to death as he sang. Although few of the Cheyenne escaped, their leader, Black Kettle, did manage to flee the scene. As he left, he carried his wife with him—she had been shot nine times but was still alive.

Plains Indians gained a measure of revenge in January 1865. Determined to exact retribution from the whites, the Cheyenne banded together with the Northern Arapaho, and the Brule and Oglala Sioux, forming a group of 1,600 handpicked warriors. This was one of the greatest cavalry units the world had ever seen, and it stormed across Colorado, severely damaging a fort, razing towns, destroying ranches, and spreading terror through the outskirts of Denver before departing. A government inquiry blamed Chivington and his men for the "barbaric" attack.

WHAT'S IN A HEADDRESS?

Judging from depictions in the media, you might assume that all Indians wore feathered headdresses. In fact, these war bonnets were worn only by Plains Indians, and only during battles and ceremonies. These pages take a look at the Plains war bonnet, along with Native headgear from other regions of North America.

Eagle feathers were added based on deeds performed by the wearer, one feather per deed.

Browbands were decorated with designs made from beads or porcupine quills.

Horse hair was often used to decorate the tips of the feathers, after the introduction of horses to the Plains.

Tassels could be made of many materials, including the tails of ermines (a type of weasel).

ARCTIC

Wooden helmet
The Aleuts used these helmets to protect their eyes from glare during kayak trips.

GREAT PLAINS

Buffalo horn bonnet
Plains warrior societies wore these during ceremonies.

NORTHEAST WOODLANDS

Roaches
Winnebago men wore these to indicate that they had killed, but not scalped, an enemy.

PACIFIC NORTHWEST

Shaman's headdress
A mask representing a spirit helper is included on this Tlingit mask.

CALIFORNIA

Feather crown
Men and women of the Maidu tribe wore these during dances.

FINAL VICTORIES, FINAL DEFEATS

By the second half of the 19th century, conditions for the Indians of the West were desperate. In spite of the odds, some tribes were determined to continue fighting for their lands and their freedom. Although there was no happy ending in store for these tribes, some did manage to achieve a few hard-won victories before their final defeat.

Red Cloud
led one of the few successful Native campaigns against white Americans, in retaliation for the establishment of the Bozeman Trail.

RED CLOUD'S WAR

In 1863, frontiersman John Bozeman established a trail that connected the well-traveled Oregon Trail with the newly discovered gold fields of Montana. For the settlers, it was a welcome shortcut, but for the Ogala Sioux, it was infuriating—the Bozeman Trail went directly through Powder River country, the last untouched bison-hunting area of the Sioux.

A few years later, in 1866, the U.S. government held a council with the Ogala to discuss the status of the Bozeman Trail. In the midst of negotiations, Red Cloud, chief of the Oglala, learned that the army was already building two new forts along the route. Furious, Red Cloud declared: "I will talk with you no more! . . . As long as I live I will fight you for the last hunting grounds of my people!" Red Cloud had his warriors use traditional Indian tactics against the intruders.

There were no direct attacks. Instead, the Sioux set free horses and mules belonging to whites. They made quick hit-and-run attacks, ambushed isolated work parties, and used snipers to pick off their enemies. As time passed, the Sioux wore down the workers and soldiers along the trail, making them constantly nervous and edgy. Hardly a day went by without one or more soldiers being killed.

Finally, in 1868, the government signed a treaty agreeing to dismantle all the forts along the Bozeman Trail. As the soldiers leaving Fort Phil Kearny looked back, they saw bands of Sioux setting fire to the buildings. It was a great triumph for Red Cloud and the Sioux. The great warrior continued fighting for his people and their lands throughout the 1870s and 1880s.

CLOSING IN ON THE SIOUX

In 1874, General George Armstrong Custer led an expedition into the Black Hills of the Dakotas. Custer was already hated by the Plains Indians for his attacks on the Southern Cheyenne, but this was an added insult because the Black Hills were sacred to the Sioux. Custer soon made things even worse by announcing that the expedition had discovered gold.

The Sioux watched in horror as gold hunters and other settlers swarmed into the Black Hills. Before Custer's expedition, there were fewer than 5,000 whites in all of Dakota Territory. Within five years the population swelled to about 134,000.

During this time, the government became determined to force the Indians of the Black Hills onto reservations. Most of the tribal leaders refused. They needed room to hunt buffalo. The government responded by sending General George Crook and a large cavalry force to make them comply.

Custer, leading a second column of troops, learned of the encampment and attacked it, without waiting for reinforcements.

In one of the most famous battles in all the Indian wars, Custer's column was surrounded by the Indians. Vastly outnumbered by as many as 1,800 Native warriors, Custer and his entire force of 225 men were killed.

TOWARD THE END

A few days later, the American people celebrated the nation's centennial—the 100th anniversary of its independence. The crowds at the Centennial Exposition in Philadelphia were stunned when the news came from Little Bighorn. For people cheering the growth and modernization of the United States, it was shocking to

CHIEF JOSEPH AND THE FLIGHT OF THE NEZ PERCE

In 1877, in response to the army's demands, Chief Joseph and the Nez Perce tribe agreed to make the move to a reservation in Idaho Territory. But when a young Nez Perce man attacked some settlers to avenge his father's death, Joseph feared retaliation. He decided to lead his band through the Bitterroot Mountains, and then north into Canada, where they would be outside the army's reach.

During the ensuing 1,700-mile (2,700 km) retreat, the Nez Perce managed to hold off the army for more than three months. Although badly outnumbered, the Nez Perce warriors evaded capture in more than a dozen engagements. In one battle, however, 89 Nez Perce were killed, 50 of them women and children.

Newspapers throughout the country told the story of the Nez Perce's journey, and many readers were sympathetic to their plight. But near the Bear Paw Mountains, just 40 miles (64 km) short of the Canadian border, the army finally forced the Indians to give up. When Joseph surrendered his ragged, starving band, he handed his rifle to the army commander and gave a statement that came to symbolize the tragedy that had befallen America's first people:

"It is cold and we have no blankets. The little children are freezing to death. My people, some of them, have run away to the hills. . . . Hear me, my chiefs. I am tired; my heart is sick and sad. From where the sun now stands I will fight no more forever."

This painted deer hide depicts the Battle of Little Bighorn from the Indian point of view.

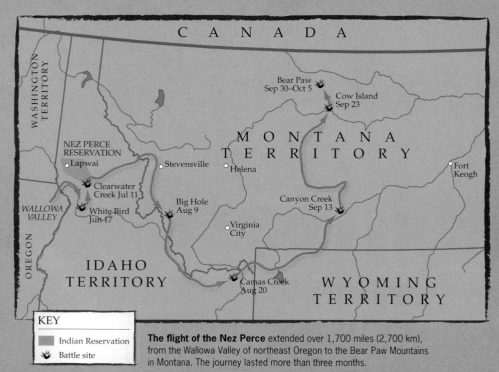

The flight of the Nez Perce extended over 1,700 miles (2,700 km), from the Wallowa Valley of northeast Oregon to the Bear Paw Mountains in Montana. The journey lasted more than three months.

THE BATTLE OF LITTLE BIGHORN

The Indians found the leader they needed for the coming showdown in Crazy Horse, a brilliant and unorthodox warrior. In June 1876, when Crook launched a three-column attack, Crazy Horse and his Oglalas stopped the southern column in a fierce battle at Rosebud Creek in southern Montana.

As Crook withdrew, Crazy Horse led his warriors to join a large Sioux and Cheyenne encampment on the Little Bighorn River, where he joined forces with Sitting Bull, another powerful Sioux leader. On June 25,

think that white Americans were still being killed by Indians in the West.

In response to public outrage, the army redoubled its efforts to force all the Indians of the West onto reservations. During this time, Sitting Bull led his people into Canada, while some Oglala continued to fight under Crazy Horse. Eventually, however, both leaders surrendered to U.S. forces, their people weakened by hunger and despair.

Chief Joseph continued to speak eloquently against the government's treatment of Native Americans, even after his surrender to the army.

Geronimo (right) and his Apache followers launched raids on Mexican and U.S. troops for many years in the late 19th century. This photo was taken after his surrender in 1886.

"CIVILIZING" THE AMERICAN INDIAN

By the late 1800s, virtually all Indian tribes had been confined to reservations. However, many Americans didn't see this as a good long-term solution to what they called the "Indian problem." Starting around 1880, the government's policy focused more and more on assimilation—the attempt to fit Indians into mainstream American life.

THE POLICY OF ASSIMILATION

The push for assimilation came from many directions. Some thought that life on the reservations was too harsh, and that assimilation provided the Indians the best chances of survival. Others simply wanted to take control of the remaining Indian land. In the late 19th century, agents of the Bureau of Indian Affairs (BIA) were given sweeping powers over reservation life. The

RESISTANCE: THE GHOST DANCE

As Indians endured the despair of life on the reservations, they looked for some way to escape or strike back. It was at this point that the Ghost Dance arrived. The Ghost Dance was developed by a Paiute prophet named Wovoka. It combined Native symbols with Christian ideas. Wovoka

This ceremonial wand was created by the Arapaho for use in the Ghost Dance. The carved face represents the owner's supernatural helper, who would have appeared in a vision experienced during an earlier performance of the dance.

arrest Chief Sitting Bull, who had fought at Little Bighorn, for failing to stop the dance. They ended up killing him instead.

Many assumed traditional Indian cultures would eventually disappear.

announced that if Native people lived righteously and performed the dance, it would bring about a new age, in which white people would no longer be a problem, and fallen Indians would rise from the dead.

Sioux medicine men carried the Ghost Dance further. They said they had special "ghost shirts" that would shield them from bullets. In late 1890, the Sioux in South Dakota began performing the Ghost Dance in great numbers, in violation of BIA rules. Many authorities saw the dance as an act of aggression and were worried the dancers might turn violent. The government sent police to

THE MASSACRE AT WOUNDED KNEE

After Sitting Bull's death, many of his people went to live with his half-brother Big Foot on another reservation. Still worried about the Ghost Dance, the army ordered Big Foot to move the newcomers and the rest of his people to a nearby fort. However, rather than follow these orders, Big Foot decided to lead his people further south, to seek shelter with the great Chief Red Cloud. On December 28, Big Foot set off with 350 of his followers. He was so ill with pneumonia that he had to be carried part of the way in a wagon. Soon, Big Foot's band was intercepted by a group of soldiers, and that night, Big Foot and his people camped by Wounded Knee Creek, surrounded by U.S. troops.

The next day, the soldiers herded the Indians into a circle and ordered them to throw down their guns. When only a few rifles were surrendered, the general ordered a search of the camp.

One of the Sioux started a Ghost Dance, and another refused to give up his gun. Standing in a circle, the 500 soldiers opened fire, tearing the camp to shreds,

Apache men, women, and children stand in line outside a government office, waiting for their weekly rations to be distributed. The provisions offered by the government were often inadequate to the people's needs.

agents banned most ceremonial dances and festivals to remove the "Indianness" of the people's lives. By 1900, Americans began speaking of the "vanishing Indian," assuming that traditional Indian cultures would eventually disappear.

using both rifles and cannons. Some of the Sioux tried to find safety in a ravine but this only made them easy targets. More than 170 Indians were killed, some of them after trying to run away. The army lost 29 men.

To the American Indians, Wounded Knee has always been a "Massacre." The famous holy man Black Elk was there a day or two after the killing. "What we saw was terrible," he later said. "Dead and wounded women and children and little babies were scattered all along where they had been trying to get away. The soldiers had followed along the gulch, as they ran and murdered them in there."

The federal government, however, was determined to portray the event as a legitimate battle—the last conflict of the Indian Wars. Accordingly, 18 soldiers of the U.S. Army were awarded the Congressional Medal of Honor. Newspaper reports supported this point of view, with statements such as, "Once more the men of the Seventh Cavalry have shown themselves to be heroes in deeds of daring."

ALLOTMENT: THE REFORMERS' MISTAKE

Allotment was another part of the government's drive to make Native Americans live the lifestyles of other Americans. The plan involved dividing reservations up into "allotments" or parcels of land, which would be privately owned by individual Indian families. To achieve this, Congress passed the Dawes Allotment Act in 1887. Under the new law, reservations could be divided into allotments of 40, 80, or 160 acres, effectively nullifying hundreds of treaties that had set aside land for the tribes.

Many Americans felt this plan was inspired by the writings of Helen Hunt Jackson, which had exposed the poverty, alcoholism, and suffering on the reservations. By giving Indian families small plots to farm, the reformers thought, they would be able to improve the quality of their lives.

Unfortunately, there were many problems with allotment. First, the plots a family received were often too small to make a living from farming. In addition, the climate and soil conditions made farming highly unpredictable. A single year of crop failure could plunge a family into hopeless poverty and make them dependent on the government.

The Wounded Knee Massacre, in which the U.S. Army opened fire on a group of Sioux, was remembered angrily by Native Americans for many years after the event. This image shows U.S. soldiers burying the Indian victims in a common grave—a particularly undignified end.

Allotment ended up costing Native Americans dearly. In 1880, about 150 million acres were under Indian title; within two generations, two-thirds of that land was held by non-Indians.

Allotment granted Indians parcels of former reservation land. Here, the U.S. allotting surveyor grants the Sioux Chief American Horse his plot. As part of the deal, Indians would also become American citizens.

ASSIMILATION THROUGH EDUCATION

In the late 1800s, many reformers thought that the best way to "civilize" the Native Americans was through education. The government established a number of schools on reservations, but children would soon be subjected to a more radical approach, in which they were entirely separated from their tribal lands.

GOING OFF THE RESERVATION

Starting in 1870, the federal government established both day schools and boarding schools on reservation land. While at school, students were forbidden from speaking their native languages or engaging in their traditional spiritual practices. However, many felt that these schools would never successfully assimilate Indian children into mainstream American society because the students were still too close to their families and cultures.

In 1879, a Civil War veteran named Richard Henry Pratt founded the Carlisle Indian Industrial School in Pennsylvania, the first federally funded Indian boarding school to be located away from a reservation. Pratt explained that the goal was to remove the children from their familiar surroundings— separating them from their family, village, food, clothing, customs, and even their language. After a few years in

Pratt's boarding school, students would be skilled in the ways of the civilized world and would find their former lives savage and repugnant. In other words, Pratt said, the new schools provided a way to "kill the Indian and save the man."

"Kill the Indian and save the man." —Richard Henry Pratt

CARLISLE INDIAN INDUSTRIAL SCHOOL

To recruit students for the first class at Carlisle, Pratt traveled to Sioux reservations on the Great Plains and returned with a trainload of 169 students. The school was

Reservation schools often made for curious juxtapositions of white and Indian cultures. Here, a camp of Sioux tipis stands before a formal white schoolhouse on the Pine Ridge Reservation in South Dakota.

Carlisle School was established with the purposes of turning Indian children into members of mainstream American society, with no attachment to their traditional customs or beliefs. This photograph shows a group of students in a math class. As was mandatory at the school, the boys have their hair cut short and both boys and girls are wearing uniforms.

operated with strict army discipline. Boys had their hair cut short. All children wore uniforms. Missionaries were brought in to teach them Christianity. Any who tried to run away were severely punished.

The boys received a vocational training that would "teach young Indians how to make a living among civilized people by practicing agricultural and mechanical pursuits." In their traditional cultures, Indian young people had been taught a communal way of life, in which everyone in the community helped the others. But now they were being taught to work and act individually, as part of a system where each person wanted to outperform everyone else.

Pratt, and those who supported him, believed that assimilation could be achieved in a generation, with Carlisle-style schools instilling Indians with the values of "civilized" society. Others felt it would be better to go more slowly, and to rely more on reservation schools. Neither approach became dominant. By 1905, there were 25 schools based on the Carlisle model with a total of just under 10,000 students, and 93 reservation boarding schools with a total of about 11,000 students.

THE RESULTS

Many students found the boarding schools to be painfully alienating. Some ran away, hundreds died of influenza or tuberculosis, and hundreds more succumbed to alcoholism or suicide. Few appreciated the school's efforts to change their way of life.

The Struggle to Adjust

1879 Luther Standing Bear was among the first class of students at the Carlisle School. From the first day at Carlisle, he had trouble adjusting. Here's how he described the process in his autobiography, *Land of the Spotted Eagle*.

"It began with the clothes. Never, no matter what our philosophy or spiritual quality, could we be civilized while wearing the moccasin and the blanket. . . . We longed to go barefoot, but were told that the dew. . . would give us colds.

Of all the changes we were forced to make, that of diet was doubtless the most injurious, for it was immediate and chaotic. . . . White bread we had for the first meal and thereafter, as well as coffee and sugar. Had we been allowed our own simple diet of meat, either boiled with soup or dried, and fruit, with perhaps a few vegetables, we should have thrived. But the change in clothing, housing, food, and confinement combined with lonesomeness was too much, and in three years nearly one half of the children from the Plains were dead."

The boarding schools also had the effect of tearing apart Indian families. Many parents were coerced into sending their children to the schools—BIA agents would often threaten to withhold food rations until they cooperated. Even during the summer, students weren't always allowed to return home. Instead, the BIA instituted a policy of "outing," in which Indians students would live with European-American families for up to three years. Nevertheless, some Carlisle graduates praised the results of their education, despite the harsh conditions.

JIM THORPE

Most Indians found the boarding schools to be little more than a nightmare, but a few emerged as successful members of mainstream American culture. The greatest of these success stories was Jim Thorpe, a graduate of Carlisle who was later named the Outstanding Male Athlete of the first half of the 20th century.

Thorpe was born in the Oklahoma Indian Territory in 1888. Although his background was racially mixed, he was raised as part of the Sauk and Fox tribe. Because of earlier schooling, Thorpe entered Carlisle as a college student. He soon proved himself to be incredibly skilled at football, as well as baseball, boxing, basketball, lacrosse, and many other sports.

Under the tutelage of Coach Glenn S. "Pop" Warner, Thorpe became an outstanding football star, leading tiny Carlisle to national prominence. In 1911 and 1912, he earned a coveted spot on the All-America team, and in the latter year he scored 25 touchdowns and 198 points. That same year, he also made a trip to Stockholm, Sweden, to compete in the Olympics. There, he achieved a feat never duplicated before or since— winning gold medals in both the decathalon and the pentathalon. At the awards ceremony, the King of Sweden called him the greatest athlete in the world.

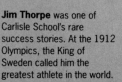

Unfortunately, Thorpe lost his gold medals when it was discovered that he had been paid for playing a few games of baseball in 1911, in violation of the Olympics' ban on professional players. The loss of the medals was devastating to Thorpe, and he never recovered emotionally from the loss. Only in 1982, years after his death, did the International Olympic Committee agree to reinstate the prizes.

Jim Thorpe was one of Carlisle School's rare success stories. At the 1912 Olympics, the King of Sweden called him the greatest athlete in the world.

BEFORE AND AFTER

The Carlisle School attempted to "civilize" Indian children by forcing them to act more like white Americans. These pictures from 1886 show a group of Chiricahua Apache children on their first day at Carlisle, and the same group four months later. Many parents were forced to send their children to Carlisle against their will.

Hair was worn long on both boys and girls, as was traditional among the Apache.

Headband was a traditional part of the Apache wardrobe. Such items were not welcome at Carlisle.

Feet were bare. The Apaches had walked barefoot through the rugged lands of the Southwest for generations.

Clothes for both boys and girls were uniform and stiff. This was thought to encourage discipline.

Hair was cut short on boys, in keeping with the customs of white society. In many Indian cultures, short hair was a sign of disgrace.

Shoes were mandatory for Carlisle students. In the eyes of white society, only "savages" went barefoot.

SURVIVAL ON THE RESERVATIONS

In the early years of the 20th century, reservation life was extremely harsh. Indians were treated as wards of the government, and the agents in charge of the reservations wielded dictatorial power. Unable to raise themselves out of poverty or to reclaim their traditional ways of life, many Indians began to lose hope.

LOSS OF LAND

One major problem facing reservations was that they were growing continually smaller due to the parceling out of land under the allotment system. Sometimes whole reservations were divided up, and other times only certain sections of the reservations were affected. Either way, the results were often devastating. When a plot of land was first given to an Indian family, the change in the land's status didn't seem to matter too much—after all, it was still in Indian hands. However, once the land was privately owned, it could eventually be acquired by non-Indians, which happened all too frequently. In addition, when an area was designated for allotment, there was often a considerable amount of land left over after all eligible Indian families had been given their share. This "surplus" land was then made available to non-Indians.

All of this contributed to a huge net loss of Indian land. What was left on the reservations was usually not enough to support a decent standard of living.

ATTACKING INDIAN CULTURES

The Indians who remained on the reservations were subject to the regulations of the government's Bureau of Indian Affairs (BIA). These regulations, enforced by officials known as Indian agents, were geared toward destroying tribal cultures and forcing Indians into the mold of mainstream American society.

Practices that were seen as too "savage" or "heathen" were banned by the agents. These prohibited practices included everything from participating in traditional dances to living in traditional homes. Often, the Indians found ways to get around these rules. For example, when the BIA demanded that Plains Indians start living in wooden houses, many left the houses empty and lived in tipis that they pitched next door.

These measures had an especially strong effect on young people, many of whom had never known life outside a reservation.

A group of Sioux women poses outside a tipi on the Pine Ridge reservation in 1891, along with an Indian policeman and U.S. marshal. In the background is a government-approved wooden house.

As a result of the government's policies, which included the forced attendance of boarding schools (see pp.148–149), young Indians were increasingly cut off from their people's history, culture, values, language, and religion.

FORCED INTO FARMING

The BIA also did its best to transform all Indians into farmers, insisting that they plant only government-approved crops, according to government-approved methods. However, Indians from farming cultures knew the methods that worked best in their conditions; they did not want to be told about the methods the BIA preferred. In addition, the planting of staples, such as corn, was closely

Corruption within the Bureau of Indian Affairs was widespread. In this political cartoon from 1890, a well-dressed Indian agent is seen carrying off huge bags of money, while an Indian is left with a parcel of food labeled "starvation rations."

INDIAN POLICE

Law and order on the reservations was maintained by Indian police—Native people trained by the government to enforce the rules. These policemen were often torn between loyalty to their people and loyalty to the agents who employed them. In the event that the Indian police were unable to handle a situation, the forces of the U.S. army were never far away.

THE MOOD OF RESERVATION INDIANS

The nation's Indians began the 20th century in a state of poverty and oppression. With little hope for the future, a growing number of Native Americans became filled with despair. Over the course of the 20th century,

Practices seen as too "savage" or "heathen" were prohibited.

tied to religious beliefs and customs for many tribes. The Hopi and Navajo believed it was a sacrilege to cut into the surface—or skin—of the earth mother. Often, the BIA regulations conflicted with these beliefs.

For Plains men in particular, the transition to farming was humiliating. Only a few years earlier, many of these Cheyennes, Arapahos, and Sioux were proud and heroic hunters, riding powerful horses across the Plains. The farm work they were being forced to do now was seen as degrading.

GOVERNMENT FOODS

Since few were able to sustain themselves through farming, the government issued food rations to most reservations. These government supplies were generally meager, and often consisted of foods that the Indians weren't accustomed to, such as cattle or pigs. One army surgeon at the Crow Creek Reservation in South Dakota described a particularly unappetizing meal, prepared in a vat of steaming water from a sawmill: "Into this vat," he wrote, "was thrown beef, beef heads, entrails of beeves, some beans, flour and pork. . . . This mass was then cooked by the steam from the boiler passing through the vat. When that was done, all the Indians were ordered to come with their pails and get it."

To make matters worse, there were many reports of government agents stealing food supplies to sell for their own profit—part of a widespread culture of corruption. As a result of poor nutrition, poor health care, and generally unsanitary conditions, diseases on the reservations were rampant.

there was a steady increase in alcoholism, mental breakdowns, and suicides on the reservations. Although conditons have improved, many of these problems are still faced by the Indians on reservations today.

Cutting it short

1897 On many reservations, agents forced all males to cut their hair short, because their long hair was a sign of "wildness." The officer in charge of getting rid of long hair on the Mescalero Apache Reservation described the process as follows.

❝ As with Samson of old, the Indians' wildness lay in their long hair, which the returned, educated Indians wore because, as they boasted, "it made them wild." All energies were bent to compel the adult males to cut their hair and adopt civilized attire in vain. . . . The Indian Office, at my request, issued a preemptory order for all to cut their hair and adopt civilized attire; and in six weeks from the start, every male Indian had been changed into the semblance of a decent man, with the warning that confinement at hard labor awaited any backsliders. ❞

REFORM EFFORTS AND SUCCESS STORIES

By the 1920s, American Indians were at a pivotal point in their history. Some Native people were achieving mainstream success, but most still lived in deplorable conditions. However, due to the efforts of reformers, a wave of sympathy for the plight of the Indians was sweeping over the country, and the government would soon begin treating them with more respect.

INDIANS IN A WHITE MAN'S WORLD

Although most Indians in the United States still lived in dire conditions, there continued to be stories of individuals breaking out of the cycle of poverty and leading successful lives in the mainstream world. One notable example was Charles Curtis. Although only one-eighth Indian, Curtis was raised by his grandmother on the Kaw Reservation and went to the reservation school. After Cheyenne warriors attacked the reservation, Curtis moved to Topeka, Kansas, where he finished high school and eventually became a lawyer.

Charles Curtis was the first person of American Indian ancestry to serve in the United States Senate. In 1924, he sponsored the Indian Citizenship Act, which made all Native Americans into citizens.

Curtis proved to have a great talent for politics. He was elected to the U.S. House of Representatives in 1892 and served eight terms, maintaining his seat until 1906. Curtis next served in the U.S. Senate, from 1907 to 1913 and again from 1915 to 1929. Finally, in 1928, Charles Curtis was elected vice president of the United States on a ticket with Republican Herbert Hoover. These were incredible achievements for someone who had grown up on a reservation. As time went on, a growing number of Indians would enjoy this kind of mainstream success.

In 1928, the average life span of an American Indian was only 44 years.

Indians in the wars

In World War I (1914–1918) and World War II (1939–1945), American Indians served with distinction alongside their countrymen. In both conflicts, some tribes used their Native languages as the basis for secret codes—the only ones never cracked by the enemy.

THE INDIAN CITIZENSHIP ACT

Prior to 1924, American Indians occupied a gray area in terms of citizenship. Unlike other Americans, they were not automatically considered citizens simply because they were born inside the borders of the United States. However, many Indians had been granted citizenship by other means. For example, an Indian could become a citizen by serving in the military, by participating in the allotment program, or by marrying an existing U.S. citizen. Furthermore, various statutes and treaties had declared certain groups of Indians to be citizens at different times and places.

Many reformers didn't like this patchwork-quilt approach to Indian citizenship. They felt that, if Indians were to be successfully assimilated into mainstream society, they should enjoy the same rights and privileges as other Americans, regardless of their personal history. Thus, in 1924, Congress passed the Indian Citizenship Act, which made all Indians full citizens of the United States.

Some American Indian groups rejected citizenship, precisely because they *didn't* want to be assimilated into mainstream

President Calvin Coolidge was responsible for signing the Indian Citizenship Act into law. Here, he poses on the White House lawn with members of the Sioux Nation in 1925.

society. This was especially true of members of the Iroquois Confederacy in New York State. These groups regarded themselves as sovereign nations, and didn't want to trade that status for citizenship in a country they didn't see themselves as belonging to. During World War II, the Iroquois again made a point of their sovereignty by declaring war on Nazi Germany, independently of the United States. In the 21st century, many Iroquois still abstain from voting in state and national elections. In addition, the Iroquois Confederacy issues passports and sends diplomats to several countries.

THE MERIAM REPORT

In 1923, a group was formed called the Committee of One Hundred. Made up of both Indians and non-Indians, the group's mission was to analyze the state of Indians in America and to lobby the government to treat them more humanely. Prominent Seneca writer Arthur C. Parker was elected presiding officer. In 1924, the committee published its findings in a report called *The Indian Problem*.

Four years later, the findings were expanded into the Meriam Report, a multivolume analysis of Indian life in America, which provided detailed information on the health, education, and living conditions of the various tribes. The report emphasized how the government, and especially the Bureau of Indian Affairs (BIA), had failed to protect the Indian people. It pointed out, for example, that hundreds of Indians were dying from diseases that had largely disappeared from the rest of the population. This was due largely to the fact that the health services on the reservations were poorly equipped and understaffed. Because of these conditions, the average life span of an Indian was only 44 years.

John Collier was an outspoken advocate of American Indian rights. In this photograph, he is shown with two Hopi men.

NEW DEAL REFORMS

When Franklin Roosevelt became president in 1933, he instituted a series of reforms known as the New Deal, designed to relieve poverty. To his credit, he did not leave American Indians out of the equation. He chose John Collier, previously an outspoken critic of BIA policies, to be the head of the agency he had long attacked. Under Collier's leadership, the BIA began changing its ways, and Congress passed the Indian Reorganization Act (IRA) of 1934.

The IRA eliminated the allotment system and its failed goal of transforming Indians into farmers. Some reservations were allowed a measure of self-government. In addition, tribes were allowed to resume their traditional ceremonies, after a half-century of repression.

The IRA also allowed tribes to vote on whether to be bound by its provisions. Over a two-year period, 181 tribes and nations accepted the IRA plan and 77 groups rejected it. The Sioux were especially vigorous in their opposition. Frank Fools Crow, a Sioux leader, argued that they were being "placed in bondage by programs we could not understand." In spite of the criticism, the IRA remained one of the 20th century's most significant reforms.

RELOCATION AND RESISTANCE

As America moved into the post-war era of the 1950s, the respect for traditional cultures that had become a part of the government's Indian policy under Roosevelt began to be replaced once again by a focus on assimilation. As always, however, many Native Americans were ready to fight back.

THE INDIAN CLAIMS COMMISSION

During World War II, Nazi Germany committed atrocious violations of human rights. When the war ended, this caused many in the United States to question their own country's treatment of minorities. One result was the creation of the Indian Claims Commission (ICC) by Congress in 1946. It was the last measure to emerge from the New Deal spirit of reform.

In the past, an Indian tribe needed special permission from Congress to sue the government for violations of treaties, especially those involving the taking of tribal lands. The ICC Act created a three-man commission to deal with all such claims. During its three decades of existence, the ICC awarded $534 million to Indian claimants, mostly in regard to land seizures. Unfortunately, the awards were based on 19th-century land values. As a result, some settlements amounted to less than a dollar per acre, far less than the tribes had hoped to receive.

RELOCATION AND TERMINATION

Despite the reform efforts of the 1920s and 1930s, conditions on Indian reservations remained extremely poor. As in the past, many non-Indians were convinced that the only solution was to bring American Indians into the mainstream of American society. By the 1950s, a majority in Congress promoted dissolving all Indian reservations as well as tribal identity and culture, a policy that became known as termination. Harsh as the program seemed, the members of Congress were convinced these steps would benefit the Indians by helping them ease their way into the modern industrial world.

Between 1954 and 1966, Congress passed laws terminating the government's recognition of 109 Indian tribes and bands. Deprived of both government aid and traditional means of support, many of these tribes simply ceased to exist, and the members moved to other communities. During this same period, the BIA launched a "relocation" program that encouraged Indians to move from reservations to cities using promises of jobs and money. However, the Indians who moved often found city life to be less fulfilling than

they'd been led to believe. Nevertheless, between 1953 and 1972, more than 100,000 American Indians made the move.

THE SEARCH FOR NEW DIRECTIONS

Most of the Indian opponents of termination and relocation were Indian traditionalists who wanted their lands restored and their cultures preserved. They were joined by urban young people—the children of those who had been relocated to cities. Starting in the 1960s, a growing number of young Indians began moving back to the reservations, disillusioned with mainstream American life.

In 1961, a group of young, college-educated Native Americans formed an organization called the National Indian Youth Council. The council had strong connections with the impoverished traditional communities, and was one of the first organizations formed to fight for American Indian rights.

That same year, John F. Kennedy, in one of his first acts as president, called for a conference of American Indians to be held to discuss their hopes for the future. Known as the American Indian Chicago Conference, it brought together more than 500 Indians representing about 60 groups. At the end of the conference, a statement

The Indian Claims Commission made it easier for tribes to settle claims with the government. Here, President Harry S. Truman signs the act that brought the commission into existence.

was issued entitled *A Declaration of Indian Purpose.* This statement proposed a new direction in federal Indian policy, in which tribal governments would have more say over what happened to the tribes.

By the mid-1960s, there was a new feeling of hope growing among American Indians. Inspired by the Civil Rights movement, which promoted the fair treatment of African-Americans and other minorities, they began to apply some of the same principles to their own situation. Over the next two decades, groups such as the National Indian Youth Council and the American Indian Movement would increasingly use protests and civil disobedience as a way of bringing attention to the problems of their people.

Indian drummers perform in the Washington state capitol in 1964, as part of a conference regarding fishing rights in Puget Sound. The protests and "fish-ins" surrounding this issue were some of the first instances of civil disobedience on the part of American Indians.

A feeling of **hope** was growing among Indians.

President John F. Kennedy speaks with representatives of the American Indian Chicago Conference, who have come to Washington to present him with their *Declaration of Indian Purpose.*

Pow-wow clothing is very colorful and often incorporates both traditional and modern elements.

CHAPTER 7
A PEOPLE'S REVIVAL

American Indians enjoy a new age of prosperity

Today, no one in North America talks about the "vanishing Indian" anymore. That's because American Indians are becoming more visible every day. In the 1960s, Indians started joining together in protests and gaining a new sense of pride. In recent years, the focus on protests has diminished, but the community spirit remains. Indians from across the country now gather at pow-wows and other events to dance, sing, and celebrate their culture—and they often have a lot to celebrate. With some tribes achieving new prosperity from casinos and other ventures, Indians are entering the 21st century with a bang.

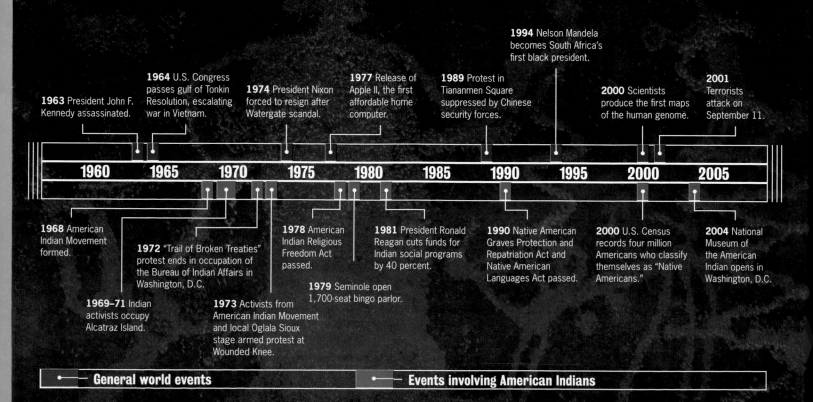

1994 Nelson Mandela becomes South Africa's first black president.

1964 U.S. Congress passes gulf of Tonkin Resolution, escalating war in Vietnam.

1977 Release of Apple II, the first affordable home computer.

1989 Protest in Tiananmen Square suppressed by Chinese security forces.

1963 President John F. Kennedy assassinated.

1974 President Nixon forced to resign after Watergate scandal.

2000 Scientists produce the first maps of the human genome.

2001 Terrorists attack on September 11.

1960 1965 1970 1975 1980 1985 1990 1995 2000 2005

1968 American Indian Movement formed.

1972 "Trail of Broken Treaties" protest ends in occupation of the Bureau of Indian Affairs in Washington, D.C.

1978 American Indian Religious Freedom Act passed.

1981 President Ronald Reagan cuts funds for Indian social programs by 40 percent.

1990 Native American Graves Protection and Repatriation Act and Native American Languages Act passed.

2000 U.S. Census records four million Americans who classify themselves as "Native Americans."

2004 National Museum of the American Indian opens in Washington, D.C.

1979 Seminole open 1,700-seat bingo parlor.

1969–71 Indian activists occupy Alcatraz Island.

1973 Activists from American Indian Movement and local Oglala Sioux stage armed protest at Wounded Knee.

● — **General world events**   ● — **Events involving American Indians**

WOUNDED KNEE REVISITED

O ver the course of the 1970s, Indian activists continued their protests, searching for ways to increase public awareness of their cause. In 1973, members of the American Indian Movement joined with Oglala Sioux activists to engage in the armed takeover of the town of Wounded Knee, South Dakota, in one of the most dramatic Native American conflicts since the 19th century.

THE INCIDENT BEGINS

In 1973, a few months after the BIA occupation, Oglala Sioux activists on the Pine Ridge Reservation in South Dakota asked for the American Indian Movement's help. Over the last several months, tribal chairman Richard Wilson had been running the reservation like a dictatorship, using his personal "goon squad" to suppress the views of anyone who disagreed with him. The Sioux activists wanted AIM to help them take a stand against Wilson.

On February 27, the combined group of activists took over the village of Wounded Knee, which was located on the reservation. Soon, a large contingent of government forces had the little town surrounded. Across the frozen fields of the Great Plains, around 200 American Indians faced a large force of federal marshals, supported by armored personnel carriers and, overhead, a squadron of fighter planes.

Oglala Sioux tribe members guard a post during the 1973 occupation of Wounded Knee. For many, the incident was a stark reminder of past injustices.

A SYMBOLIC STANDOFF

At the time, the name Wounded Knee was already familiar to many Americans—it had been the site of the famous 1890 massacre, in which 300 Sioux had been ruthlessly killed by the U.S. Army (see p.146). In 1970, author Dee Brown had published a best-selling book called *Bury My Heart at Wounded Knee,* which told the story of the West from the

Indian point of view, causing the phrase "Wounded Knee" to be even more strongly implanted in people's minds.

AIM was of course well aware of this when they decided to take over the town. Their goal was not just to get rid of Richard Wilson, but to bring national attention to the plight of American Indians. Once federal troops moved in, the internal tribal conflict that had prompted the takeover fell into the background.

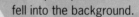

When people across the country watched the incident on television, they saw only a standoff between Indians and whites, at a place called Wounded Knee. The symbolic power was difficult to ignore.

the government's actions at Wounded Knee, as well as the unfair depiction of Indians in television and movies. This directed even more attention toward the ongoing standoff at the town.

The symbolic power was difficult to ignore.

The occupation ended up lasting for 71 day, making headlines across the country. The impact was often dramatic. In March, for example, actor Marlon Brando won an Academy Award for his role in *The Godfather*, but he didn't show up to accept it. Instead, he sent an AIM activist named Sacheen Littlefeather to decline the award on his behalf. She explained that Brando was refusing the award as a way of protesting

THE AFTERMATH

Toward the end of the occupation, the media paid almost no attention. When it came to an end in early May, there were no clear winners or losers. Two Indians had been killed, a U.S. marshal had been paralyzed, and the Sioux village of Wounded Knee was in ruins.

AIM was discredited and never recovered. The government spent more than two years tracking down every Indian occupier they could find and prosecuting them in court. Dennis Banks and Russell Means each faced five charges, carrying penalties totaling 85 years, but the charges were eventually dismissed. In 1974, Means, himself an Oglala Sioux, ran against Richard Wilson for the position of tribal chairman but lost by about 200 votes.

This poster explicitly associates the 1890 Wounded Knee Massacre with the 1973 occupation. Many AIM leaders encouraged this way of thinking with their speeches and actions.

Russell Means (center) and Dennis Banks (right) confer with Civil Rights leader Ralph Abernathy during the Wounded Knee occupation.

MURDER MYSTERIES AND LEGAL BATTLES

During the last quarter of the 20th century, American Indians continued to fight for their rights. Increasingly, their battles took place in the courtroom. In some cases, the government brought charges against Indians, and in others, the situation was reversed.

THE CASE OF LEONARD PELTIER

Leonard Peltier, a member of the Anishinabe and Dakota tribes, had been an AIM activist during the 1973 confrontation at Wounded Knee. In June 1975, he was caught in a shootout with the FBI and state police on the Pine Ridge Reservation. Soon afterward, he was charged with the killing of two FBI agents.

Over the course the trial, which was held in Fargo, North Dakota, many became convinced that Peltier was not getting a fair hearing. The prosecution's main witness, Myrtle Poor Bear, had her testimony contradicted by several other witnesses. When she asked for a chance to withdraw her testimony, the judge refused her request. Critics also pointed out that the prosecution had taken five weeks to present its case, while the defense was stopped after only three. There were no eyewitnesses who could name Peltier as the shooter.

Peltier was convicted and sentenced to life in prison. For the next two decades, his supporters agitated for a new trial, but his appeals were turned down again and again. By the 1990s, the demand for a retrial had became a worldwide crusade, with millions signing petitions of support.

Early in 1994, a five-month walk was held on behalf of Peltier, involving about 400 people. Twenty-eight ended up walking the full 3,000-mile (4,828 km) distance, finishing in Washington, D.C. There, the protesters appealed to President Bill Clinton to grant a pardon to Peltier, but Clinton ultimately refused.

While in prison, Peltier has been involved in many projects to better the lives of American Indians on the outside. He has worked with physicians to improve health care on the reservations. He has worked on various job programs, including one dedicated to teaching young people on

Leonard Peltier evaded arrest for several months, and was eventually captured in Canada. Here, Canadian authorities lead him to a helicopter, which is waiting to take him back to the United States.

reservations how to start and operate their own businesses. An accomplished artist, Peltier donates his artwork to the Leonard Peltier Charitable Foundation, which provides computers, books, and supplies to Pine Ridge Reservation schools. Meanwhile, supporters across the globe continue to petition for his release.

THE DEATH OF ANNA MAE AQUASH

In the three years following the occupation of Wounded Knee, more than 60 people were killed on the Pine Ridge Reservation, giving it one the highest murder rates in the country. At the time, there was a great amount of tension between the supporters of AIM and supporters of Richard Wilson, and many think the killings may have been politically motivated.

In February 1976, a rancher found the body of Anna Mae Aquash at Pine Ridge. Born into the MicMac tribe of Nova Scotia, Canada, Aquash had been a prominent member of AIM, and a close friend of Peltier, Banks, and Means. The BIA's pathologist said she had died of exposure in the bitter Great Plains winter.

Due to problems with identification, Aquash's family was not informed of her death until after she was buried. Once they learned the news, they could not accept that she had died of exposure. She had been young, in great shape, and trained to survive cold weather. They demanded a new autopsy. After her body was exhumed, a new pathologist found a bullet at the base of her skull. How could the BIA pathologist have

The Return of Dennis Banks

After being convicted of riot charges in South Dakota in 1973, AIM leader Dennis Banks eluded capture for many years. At first he remained in hiding, but he later lived openly in California—Governor Jerry Brown had granted him amnesty and refused to turn him over to South Dakota authorities. In 1985, Banks surrendered and served 18 months in prison. Since his release, he has worked as a counselor on the Pine Ridge Reservation and acted in several films.

missed such an obvious clue? No one seemed to have an answer.

The Canadian government and the U.S. Commission on Civil Rights demanded an investigation. The Justice Department agreed to conduct one but then delayed again and again. Tribal members wrapped Aquash's body in a traditional star quilt, and the women mourned for two days and nights.

In 2003, 27 years after Aquash's death, two men named Arlo Looking Cloud and John Graham were charged with her murder. Although Looking Cloud was convicted in 2004, it is still not clear what the motivation was for the killing.

HALF THE FISH IN WASHINGTON

In the 1850s, tribes in Washington State had been assured the right to fish on their traditional waters without government regulation. By the mid-20th century, however, the state government no longer recognized this right. Starting in 1964, these tribes held "fish-ins," during which they fished without permission from the state. Often, these fish-ins led to the arrest of the Native fishermen, and the confiscation of their boats and nets.

In 1974, the Washington tribes scored a major victory, when a federal judge declared that the government could not interfere with the Indians' right to fish, and that the tribes were entitled to half of all the fish in the state. Unfortunately, this decision caused a backlash against the Indians by some non-Native fishermen, who felt that the Indians were being given an unfair advantage. Today, the Indians and the state government serve as equal partners in the magagement of the the state's fishing resources.

VICTORIES IN THE COURTS

As the 1970s came to a close, Native Americans continued to use the legal process to restore the rights and independence of their tribes. In one of the most famous cases, two tribes, the Passamaquoddy and the Penobscots, proved that they were the legal owners of most of the state of Maine. After this verdict was declared in 1980, the state offered a settlement: 300,000 acres of land and a cash payment of $27.5 million. The tribes eventually agreed to accept.

More court cases followed. Some involved land claims, others involved tribal rights to regulate resources, and some involved the status of gambling on reservations. The following pages look at how some of these cases led to sweeping changes in the fortunes of the tribes.

Two tribes proved they owned most of the state of Maine.

A young Nez Perce man demonstrates a traditional salmon fishing technique. Fishing rights are an important issue for many North American tribes.

Indian activists detain government officials and farmers who were trying to enter the town, during the 1973 Wounded Knee Incident. The captives were released after about an hour.

THE PROMISE OF THE CASINO

As they move into the 21st century, American Indians continue to face many of the same issues that they've struggled with for years. Poverty remains one of the most severe problems. In the search for solutions, many tribes have started operating casinos. Although this strategy has proved hugely effective in some cases, not all Native people have shared in the success.

Indian casinos have provided huge profits for certain tribes, but many others have been left behind. Operated by the San Carlos Apache Nation in Arizona, the Apache Gold Casino features slot machines, blackjack, bingo, as well as dining at the Apache Grill and Wickiup Buffet.

CONTINUING POVERTY

While some progress is being made in reducing reservation poverty, it remains one of the most pressing Indian problems. The Pine Ridge Reservation, for example, entered the 21st century as the poorest region in the country. During the 1990s, the reservation's infant mortality rate was three times the national average, and the death rate from alcoholism was four times the national average. According to the 2000 Census, more than half the reservation's children lived below the poverty line, meaning that their families' didn't make enough money to support an adequate standard of living.

Many reservations In the United States are isolated from the mainstream of American life. They have no bus or railroad connections to larger communities. Many have no movie theaters or banks, and no stores besides small grocery shops.

Conditions are similar on Canadian reservations. The Cree-Ojibwe reservation of Pikangikum in Ontario has an 80 percent unemployment rate and what may be the highest suicide rate in the world. Tribal elders point out that there is little in the area for young people to do. "When they're not sleeping, they're out roaming and sniffing [glue]," said one elder. Many young Indians end up joining gangs and abusing drugs.

THE GROWTH OF RESERVATION GAMBLING

Over the last few decades, more and more U.S. tribes have started using casinos to bring much-needed revenue to their people. Before European contact, a love of gambling was common to many Native peoples. This generally took the form of simple games, such as tossing marked sticks or a polished stones. Game play almost always involved luck, rather than skill.

In the modern era, Indians have been able to establish gambling operations due to the unique legal status of reservations. In most U.S. states, gambling is prohibited or heavily restricted. However, reservations are generally not subject to these laws. As a result, tribes are allowed to open casinos on reservation land, and these are often the only casinos in the area. This ensures them a steady stream of loyal patrons, who would otherwise have to travel to Las Vegas or Atlantic City to play their favorite games.

The Pine Ridge Reservation in South Dakota is one of the poorest regions of the country. Here, Leon Brave Heart, a 22-year-old Oglala Sioux man, sits outside the Pine Ridge trailer he calls home.

The idea of using gambling to bring revenue to Indian tribes first emerged in the late 1970s. In 1979, the Seminole opened a bingo parlor with 1,700 seats and prizes of $10,000. The enterprise was so successful that they began building more bingo halls, as well as some casinos. Other groups soon followed the trend. Within 10 years, the Congressional Research Service reported that more than 100 reservations had some form of gambling, with annual revenues of more than $250 million.

SIGNS OF SUCCESS

By the year 2000, a number of once-impoverished reservations were reaping huge benefits from their gambling operations. For example, in 1992, the Shakopee-Mdewakanton Sioux established a casino on their reservation outside the city of Minneapolis. The tribe, which had barely 100 members, quickly began collecting enormous profits. By 1996 each member was receiving an average of $2,000 a month from the casino. In addition, the profits allowed everyone in the tribe to have access to health insurance, a guaranteed job, and a full college scholarship.

Perhaps the most successful of all Indian casinos is Foxwoods Resort Casino in Connecticut. Opened by the Pequot in 1992, Foxwoods includes 7,400 slot machines, 380 gaming tables, and a 3,000-seat high-stakes bingo parlor with $1 million jackpots. It is the biggest casino in the world, as measured by floor space devoted to gaming, and the voluntary contributions made by the casino's management now make up a significant part of the state's budget.

SIGNS OF OPPOSITION

All this success has not come without controversy. One problem is that the huge profits generated by gambling can lead to

Opposition to casinos is common in many Indian tribes. The Mohawk nation, whose lands straddle the border between the United States and Canada, is involved in a particlarly bitter ongoing dispute.

corruption. In some cases, people have been expelled from tribes under dubious circumstances in order to concentrate wealth in the hands of the remaining members. For example, in 1995, some members of the Oneida nation, which operates a large casino, took part in a "march for democracy," protesting the leadership of the nation's representative, Raymond Halbritter.

Shortly afterward, Halbritter informed the protesters that they were no longer considered members of the tribe. Many American Indians saw an ominous message in the Oneida's experience: Casinos could be very profitable for Native people, but that success could lead to the loss of democracy and the concentration of power in the hands of a dictator.

Some Indian leaders have also argued that gambling will weaken the people of the tribe. They fear that tribe members will become addicted to gambling, or else become lazy

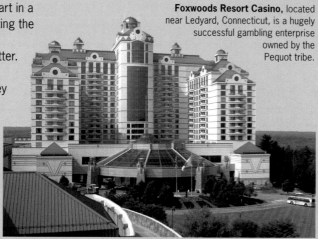

Foxwoods Resort Casino, located near Ledyard, Connecticut, is a hugely successful gambling enterprise owned by the Pequot tribe.

due to the easy income flowing in from the casinos. Another problem with gambling is that it has created the false sense that all Indian societies are now prosperous. A few tribes and nations have indeed become very successful, but the majority of reservations continue to struggle with poverty and other issues. With so much attention being paid to Indian success stories, these problems run the risk of being ignored.

THE BALANCE SHEET TODAY

Today, there are approximately 400 Indian gambling establishments in the United States, operated by 220 tribes. The total revenue brought in by these operations is nearly $18.5 billion. After paying operating costs, the tribal governments use much of the profits to improve the infrastructure of the reservations—building much-needed health clinics, schools, day-care centers, roads, and sewage systems.

The revenues also give the tribes the ability to invest in other businesses, such as convention centers and spas. By diversifying in this way, tribal leaders hope that, in time, the reservations will not be as dependent on gaming.

In addition, many tribes with high casino revenues offer assistance to tribes that are still struggling, and also donate to nonprofit organizations such as the Special Olympics. In 2004, according to the National Indian Gaming Association, the casino tribes provided more than $100 million in such assistance. For better or for worse, it is clear that casinos have radically altered the position of Indian tribes within the fabric of American society.

NATURAL RESOURCES AND ANCIENT RELICS

American Indians have always had a strong connection to the land. In the modern world, this connection has become more complicated. Many tribes are now reaping profits from the land's oil and mineral resources, while others are fighting for the return of relics that were dug up from the ground long ago.

OIL AND THE NAVAJO

Indian reservations account for only about three percent of the land area of the United States. However, this land potentially contains up to 25 percent of the nation's mineral resources, including 10 percent of the oil and natural gas, 33 percent of the low-sulfur coal, and up to half of the uranium that is not on other government-controlled land.

For the greater part of their history, most tribes gained little from this mineral wealth. The BIA had negotiated many mineral contracts with the Native people, but always in ways that benefited private companies at the expense of the Indians. For example, oil was discovered on the Navajo Reservation in 1921, but most of the profits went to the oil companies, with little ending up in Navajo hands.

This was unfortunate, since the Navajo were in desperate need of money. Ever since the 1860s, their reservation had suffered through decade after decade of poverty. Often, they had to depende on the help of emergency government funds, such as those provided by the 1950 Navajo-Hopi Long-Range Rehabilitation Act, which allocated $90 million for the building of roads, schools, and hospitals on Navajo and Hopi lands.

In the 1970s, the Navajo were finally able to renegotiate their oil contracts so they would get more money. With the added revenue, the tribe became increasingly self-sufficient. They even invested in new businesses, such as tourism, trucking, and outlets for Navajo and Hopi crafts.

URANIUM: THE NEGATIVE IMPACT

Uranium is a radioactive element, which is used in the production of both nuclear power and nuclear weapons. In the late 1940s, uranium was discovered on Navajo land, and soon the reservation was home to more than 1,000 mines, accounting for nearly 80 percent of U.S. uranium production. At a time when the tribe's economic outlook was still grim, many Navajo men jumped at the chance to work in the mines.

The Navajo were largely unaware of the severe risks associated with exposure to uranium. As they went about their work, the miners were exposed to huge amounts of radiation—up to 1,000 times the amount considered safe. By 1970, about 200 miners had died of radiation-related illnesses. By the time the government began shutting down the uranium mines in the 1980s, hundreds more had become sick.

To make matters worse, the mining operations often ended up contaminating the environment, affecting many Navajo who had never set foot near a mine. This

Coal mines like this are a common sight on the Navajo Reservation. In recent decades, the Navajo have become more self-sufficient due largely to profits from their mineral resources.

was mainly due to the heaps of waste products that were left in the area. When uranium is first dug out of the ground, it is in a form known as ore, in which it is mixed with other minerals. When the uranium is extracted, more than 95 percent of the ore is left over. On the Navajo reservation, this waste was stored in mesa-like heaps near the mines. One pile measured 70 feet (21 m) high and 1 mile (1.6 km) long. The dust from these heaps blew into nearby communities and water supplies, but the government's Atomic Energy Commission assured everyone that it was safe.

Not until the 1990s did the government admit the dangers caused by the mining operations. By this time, the death toll among former miners had reached 450, and was still growing. A few former miners and their families received compensation of $100,000, but many payments were blocked by bureaucratic delays.

CULTURAL CONCERNS

Not all tribes think selling their mineral resources is a good idea. For example, the Northern Cheyenne reservation in southeastern Montana is located on top of several billion tons of coal, which could generate much wealth. However, in recent years the tribe has refused to allow any coal mining on their land. Like most other tribes, the Northern Cheyenne believe the earth is sacred, and they feel that digging up the land in a strip-mining operation would be a violation of their beliefs.

Many Indians also feel that large-scale mining brings too many non-Indians onto the reservation. This creates pressure on social services, housing, medical facilities, and schools. Finally, a number of tribes have resisted signing mining or drilling contracts out of fear of being exploited.

RESTORING RELICS

Indian lands also contain other kinds of resources, which have not traditionally been governed by contracts. These are the cultural relics that have been removed by non-Indian collectors and scientsts.

In the past, private collectors and museums often helped themselves to objects of beauty or historical importance,

Uranium mines are hazardous even after they're abandoned. However, with time and effort, they can be made safe again, or "reclaimed." This man holds two Pueblo pots made out of clay from a reclaimed mine.

regardless of where they were found. Over the years, more than two million American Indian artifacts, including human remains and burial offerings, have been stored in museums, historical societies, private warehouses, and universities. In addition, the Smithsonian Institution holds about 800,000 such objects.

Many Indians are angry that these artifacts have been held by non-Indian groups for so long—especially the human remains. Walter and Roger Echo-Hawk, representing the Pawnee, wrote: "If you desecrate a white grave, you end up sitting in prison. But desecrate an Indian grave, you get a Ph.D. The time

has come for people to decide: are we Indians part of this country's living culture, or are we just here to supply museums with dead bodies?"

In 1989, Congress approved funding for the Smithsonian's National Museum of the American Indian, which opened in Washington, D.C., in 2004. At part of the package, they included provisions for returning certain relics and human remains held by the Smithsonian, so that tribes could reclaim their most treasured objects.

The following year, another congressional measure, known as the Native American Graves Protection and Repatriation Act, empowered Indian groups to reclaim items from other museums throughout the country. The process of having an object returned is a long and complicated one, but American Indians now enter the process with the law firmly on their side.

Since 1989, the National Museum of the American Indian has returned about 2,000 objects to more than 100 Native communities. Progress has been slow, however, because there has been a good deal of opposition to restoring human remains—many scholars argue that the they should be kept for future scientific study. As with so many issues relating to American Indians, these debates are unlikely to be resolved anytime soon.

The Disaster at Church Rock

In July 1978, one of the worst radioactive accidents in U.S. history occurred near the Navajo town of Church Rock, New Mexico. More than 1,000 tons of uranium waste products gushed through a break in a packed-earth dam, along with 100 million gallons (379 million liters) of radioactive water. Three hours later, measurements at Gallup, New Mexico, 50 miles (80 km) away, revealed the river radioactivity levels to be 6,000 times the allowable levels. A month later, only 50 tons of the spilled waste had been cleaned up. The company that owned the dam posted warnings not to drink the water, but many residents could not read English.

The Northern Cheyenne see strip mining as a violation of their beliefs.

SPORTS MASCOTS AND OTHER SYMBOLS

MASCOT PROTEST PIN

Some of America's best-loved sports teams feature Indian mascots. However, many American Indians see these mascots as profoundly disrespectful to their culture. In the modern age, this kind of symbolic issue has become an important part of the Native American struggle to be treated with dignity and respect.

A MATTER OF DIGNITY

Many American Indians feel that they have been pushed to the edges of American society. Too often, the only depictions of Indians that most Americans see are crude caricatures based on stereotypes. Nowhere is this more true than in the area of sports mascots. From the Cleveland Indians to the Atlanta Braves, professional sports is filled with references to Indians. In addition, hundreds of schools and colleges have used Indian names.

Many real Indians say that the use of these names and mascots takes away their sense of self-worth and dignity. They feel that it reinforces the idea that Indians are not much more than cartoons. In a 2001 survey conducted by the newspaper *Indian Country Today,* 81 percent of Native Americans polled felt this use of Indian names and symbols was "deeply offensive." The paper pointed out that reducing people to cartoons or mascots made it easier to ignore their major concerns. Over the

Chief Wahoo is the mascot for the Cleveland Indians baseball team. The use of the character has been the subject of many protests in recent years.

The tomahawk chop is beloved by fans of the Atlanta Braves, but many American Indians would like to see it get the ax.

Indian mascots are still used by hundreds of schools across the United States, although their use has declined in recent years.

Emotions run high on both sides of the issue. Many fans and players are strongly attached to these mascots, and don't want to change symbols that have been in place for decades. On the other hand, it would be unthinkable in today's society to use an African-American stereotype as a mascot, so why should it be any different for Indians?

THE BIG HOLDOUTS

The Washington Redskins football team remains one of the main targets of Indian anger and protest. The term *Redskin* is widely regarded as a distasteful slur. As one court statement said, the word has "a tendency to bring Native Americans into contempt or disrepute." In spite of the protests, the Washington Redskins have kept their name.

Another high-profile team that has refused to change is baseball's Atlanta Braves. (*Brave* is an outdated term for an Indian warrior.) Indians often express the greatest anger over the "tomahawk chop"—a cheer in which the crowd bellows an imitation war chant while menacingly swinging foam tomahawks. In 1991, the Braves traveled to Minneapolis for the World Series. They were met at the stadium by several hundred protestors, with signs reading, "500 Years of Oppression is Enough!" Since that time, the protests have continued, but, like the Redskins, the Braves have shown no inclination to change.

The word *squaw* has been banned from place names by some states because many find it offensive. Here, an employee of Maine places a sign for Big Squaw township into storage after the passage of such a law.

a part of the country's geographic vocabulary for so long that it is now far removed from any of its original meanings.

SYMBOLISM OF WOUNDED KNEE

In 1990, 100 years after the massacre at Wounded Knee, representatives of South Dakota's Indian tribes sat in the rotunda of the state capitol at Pierre, smoking a ceremonial peace pipe with the governor. This symbolic act was part of the governor's "year of reconciliation" between the state and its American Indian citizens.

The governor, however, refused to support the one act of reconciliation the Indians most wanted: a request that the federal government revoke the 24 Medals of Honor that had been awarded to soldiers for their actions at Wounded Knee in 1890 (see pp.146–147).

Mario Gonzalez, an attorney for the Indians, said that the government should "stand tall, admit it was wrong, and atone for that massacre."

For Indians throughout North America, Wounded Knee continues to be a symbol of the government's brutal actions toward Indians. At least 300 Sioux were killed that day, including women and children who were trying to run away. The Sioux insist that the government added to the crime by granting the highest Congressional honor to the soldiers involved. So far, the medals have not been revoked.

Many Indians feel these mascots are deeply offensive.

PROGRESS IS MADE

The first changes came in the early 1970s, partly in response to campaigns started by AIM in the Midwest. They started with the University of Nebraska at Omaha, which switched from the Indians to the Mavericks. Stanford University was next, switching over from the Indians to the Cardinals.

From the 1970s on, the campaign to change team names gained momentum. Since that time, roughly two-thirds of the nation's 3,000 elementary schools, high schools, and colleges with Indian names or mascots have replaced them. A number of "big name" athletic schools have also changed team names. Milwaukee's Marquette University, for example, replaced their Warriors with Golden Eagles. And at Seattle University, the Chieftains were exchanged for the Redhawks.

REMOVING 'SQUAW' FROM PLACE NAMES

The word *squaw*, which refers to an American Indian woman, is considered by many to be very offensive. However, there are currently more than 1,000 places in the United States whose names contain the word. In 1995, a number of Indians, including several high school students, persuaded the state of Minnesota to issue a ban on the use of the word in place names throughout the state. Squaw Lake became Nature Lake, and Squaw Point became Oak Point. Since then, there have been similar efforts in other states. Opponents say that the movement is meaningless, claiming that the word has been

MEDAL OF HONOR

years, nearly 100 organizations, including non-Indian groups such as the American Psychological Association and the National Education Association, have supported the elimination of Indian mascots.

A NEW AGE OF PRIDE AND PROGRESS

North America's Native people have come a long way since the days of the "vanishing Indian." Motivated by a sense of pride in their people, many groups have made great progress in revitalizing their cultures—showing the world that American Indians are here to stay.

RETRIBALIZATION IN VIRGINIA

For most of the 20th century, the state of Virginia only recognized two Indian tribes, the Pamunkey and Mattaponi. However, there were many other Indian groups throughout the state that were not recognized by either the state or federal government. Starting in the 1980s, these groups began petitioning for state recognition, and six have now been officially embraced by the state.

For the tribes, this process is part of a larger movement known as retribalization, in which Indian groups seek to re-establish and revitalize their tribal identities. Over the last 20 years, these Virginia tribes have worked actively to restore all aspects of their traditional cultures, including customs, ceremonies, foods, and religious beliefs. Like other tribes and nations, they hold pow-wows to share their culture with Indians and non-Indians. They are also striving to revive their original Algonquian language, which has not been spoken for roughly 200 years.

NEZ PERCE TRADITIONS

On the Nez Perce reservation in Idaho, the past and future seem to live side by side. Many tribe members operate their own businesses in fields such as construction and landscaping. Others work at casinos or stores. However, despite leading modern lifestyles, the Nez Perce also increasingly engage in many traditional festivals, such as First Fruits and First Salmon, which give thanks for the food that nature provides.

One of the most prominent of these revitalized traditions involves the breeding of their famous Appaloosa horses. Although horses were unknown in North America before the arrival of the Europeans, the Nez Perce acquired the animals early, around 1700, and soon developed a distinctive spotted breed. In the early 1800s, Meriwether Lewis called the Appaloosas "lofty, elegantly formed, active, and durable."

In 1994, the Nez Perce established a reservation horse program dedicated to teaching young people about tribal history, as well as horse breeding, training, and sales. People of all ages compete in horse shows and rodeos. In 1998, Nez Perce horse breeders developed a new breed of Appaloosa, which has given a great boost to the business.

Another source of pride for the Nez Perce is the heroic journey led by Chief Joseph in 1877 (see p141). In 1986, Congress added the Nez Perce National Historic Trail to the nation's trail system, marking the path of the historic leader's flight.

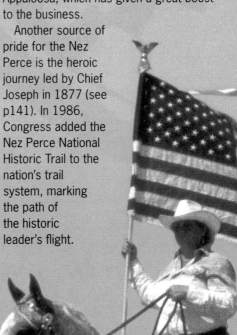

The Nez Perce National Historic Trail was established in 1986. This sign includes the word *nee-me-poo*, meaing "the people," which the Nez Perce use to refer to themselves.

NORTHERN REVIVAL

The Inuit and Aleut struggled against severe poverty through much of the 20th century. After 1970, however, there was considerable improvement as the people regained land and began receiving increased government aid. In 1971, the United States awarded 44 million acres of land to the Native peoples of Alaska, along with nearly $1 billion. In Canada, entire villages of low-cost housing were erected in Inuit areas, and in 1999, the Inuit-majority province of Nunavut was established in the north of the country, giving the Native people a greater voice in their government.

Most Inuit today live in modern houses, motor vehicles have replaced dogsleds, and food and clothing are bought from stores. At the same time, there is a strong emphasis on traditional languages and skills. Some Inuit artists have become world famous for their works in bone, ivory, and soapstone. Today, young people are learning exactly the same crafts.

LANGUAGE REVIVAL

One important way American Indians are revitalizing their cultures is by studying their traditional languages. Tribal leaders are convinced that this helps to preserve a tribe's traditions and values, and many tribes have launched ambitious language programs. The Cherokee language (see pp.128–129) is taught in many communities, often in the form of language immersion programs, in which Cherokee is the only language spoken. Similar programs have also been established by other tribes.

POPULATION AND PRIDE

Over the last few decades, the number of Indians counted by the U.S. Census has grown enormously. From 1970 to 2000, the number grew from 800,000 to more than 4,000,000. This huge increase is due largely to the fact that more people of Native heritage are identifying themselves as Indian—a clear

Pow-Wows

One of the most visible signs of the revitalization of Indian cultures is the popularity of the pow-wow, a gathering in which Indians of many tribes come together to celebrate their culture. The central event of the pow-wow is the dance competition. During this contest, dancers perform in colorful clothing, accompanied by drums and singing. The dancers' outfits can incorporate traditional designs or innovative new looks, depending on the style of the dance. Often, significant prize money is awarded to the winner.

Nez Perce riders on Appaloosa horses make a ceremonial journey along the Nez Perce trail to commemorate the famous flight.

RELATIONS BETWEEN THE CULTURES

Over the last few decades, non-Indians have become increasingly interested in Indian culture. Native art adorns homes across the continent, people of all races attend pow-wows, and many have been inspired by the philosophies of various tribes. At the same time, depictions of Indians in the mainstream media have grown more positive, leading to a greater understanding of Indian ways.

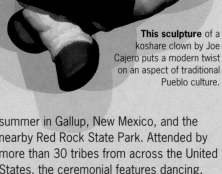

This sculpture of a koshare clown by Joe Cajero puts a modern twist on an aspect of traditional Pueblo culture.

EVOLVING ARTWORK

Throughout the United States and Canada, Indian arts and crafts continue to grow in popularity. In the Southwest, Navajo women weave blankets according to traditional techniques, and their products fetch high prices at stores across the region. In Alaska and Canada, Inuit artists create beautiful carvings in soapstone, bone, or ivory, which are sold in upscale stores throughout the world.

In addition, many acclaimed Indian artists have blended traditional motifs

Navajo blankets are still in great demand in American culture. Here, a Navajo woman weaves a blanket on a traditional upright loom.

with their own innovations to create bold new styles. For example, starting in the 1920s, at San Ildefonso Pueblo, a number of husband-and-wife teams became known for their pottery. Probably the most famous couple, Maria and Julian Martinez, developed a style that garnered international attention for its reflective "black-on-black" color scheme.

Around this same time, a group of Kiowa painters known as the Kiowa Five developed a striking visual style that was inspired by the drawings their ancestors had made in ledger books while imprisoned by the U.S. Army. Their paintings, which used vivid planes of color to depict traditional dances and myths, became famous throughout the world, demonstrating that, in addition to making traditional crafts, American Indians could become successful as "serious" artists as well.

Many artists followed in their footsteps. Today, American Indian art includes the traditional, the experimental, and everything in between. In addition, the Native American community includes many respected writers, such as Louise Erdrich, Sherman Alexie, and Leslie Marmon Silko, whose novel *Ceremony* is often found on reading lists for both high-school and college classes. There are also many Native scholars and critics, and several Native-run academic journals. Through their talent and determination, these artists and scholars have helped create greater understanding between Indian and non-Indian cultures.

POW-WOWS AND MORE

The cultural influence of American Indians can be seen in areas besides artwork as well. Every year, more and more non-Indians attend pow-wows and other Indian events. One of the most popular is the Gallup Inter-Tribal Ceremonial, held every summer in Gallup, New Mexico, and the nearby Red Rock State Park. Attended by more than 30 tribes from across the United States, the ceremonial features dancing, music, food markets, parades, rodeos, and programs that provide information about Indian ways of life.

THE ENVIRONMENTAL ETHIC

One aspect of Native culture that has received special attention in recent years is the Indian attitude toward the environment. In most Indian societies, great importance was placed on the careful management of natural resources. Most tribes never killed any plant or animal unless it was necessary for their survival, and sought to live in harmony with the natural world.

Over the last 50 years, its has become obvious that many aspects of our modern lifestyle are causing severe damage to the environment. In searching for solutions, many environmentalists have turned toward American Indian ideas. In his 1963 book *The Quiet Crisis*, Secretary of the Interior Stewart L. Udall wrote: "It is ironical today that the conservation movement finds itself turning back to ancient Indian land ideas, to the Indian understanding that we are not outside of nature, but of it. From this wisdom we can learn how to conserve the best parts of our continent."

HEALING AND CHILD-REARING

There are many other ways in which Indian societies can teach non-Indians by example. In the 20th century, psychiatrists began studying methods used by Indian healers, noting that some curing ceremonies seemed to be designed to address the mental state of the sick person, rather than just the physical ailment. Child psychologists have also studied Indian methods of raising children, which often put more emphasis on positive reinforcement than on punishment. Today, these kinds of approaches have become popular in many mainstream American circles—another example of American Indians paving the way.

DEPICTIONS IN THE MEDIA

Many non-Indians base their ideas of Native Americans on what they see in movies and on television. Unfortunately, for most of the 20th century, what they saw were inaccurate stereotypes, which offered false ideas about Indian history and culture. In countless Western movies, Indians were depicted as savage killers, ready to scalp the white heroes at a moment's notice. Filmmakers generally paid little attention to the accuracy of Indian clothing or cultural practices, and situations were rarely presented from the Indian point of view.

Luckily, this has started to change in recent years. Movies such as 1990's *Dances with*

Little Big Man, a 1970 movie starring Dustin Hoffman, contained many historical inaccuracies but was one of the first films to tell the story of the West from the Indian perspective.

Wolves and 2007's *Bury My Heart at Wounded Knee* depict Indians in a sympathetic and more realistic light, wearing the right clothes and speaking the right languages. Also, Indian roles are increasingly being played by Indian actors, giving America's first people the opportunity to help tell their own story to the world.

Dancers from the San Juan pueblo perform the Buffalo Dance at the Gallup Inter-Tribal Ceremonial.

The Gallup Inter-Tribal Ceremonial features many forms of American Indian dancing. Here, a group of San Juan Pueblos perform the eagle dance.

WHAT DOES THE FUTURE HOLD?

Since the arrival of Europeans on the continent, American Indians have survived an endless array of challenges: epidemic diseases, land-hungry settlers, and efforts to stamp their cultures out of existence. What does the future hold for the many diverse groups? Can they continue to maintain the balance between the old world and the new, or will the pull of modern society lead them to abandon their traditional ways of life?

THE MIXING OF LIFESTYLES

American Indians have made remarkable progress over the last 50 years. After centuries of hardship, they have regained some areas of their tribal lands and restored some elements of their cultures. Businesses such as casinos and mining have brought significant revenues to more than 100 reservations, from New England to the Plains to the Southwest.

To a certain extent, Native people can now choose to live traditional lifestyles on reservations, or move to cities or suburbs and live much as mainstream Americans do. But if more American Indians choose to live away from their tribal lands, won't they gradually lose touch with their traditions and fellow tribe members? For many tribal elders, this is a growing problem—they sometimes refuse to admit young people into traditional orders because their lifestyles are too modern. However, others are more optimistic. Mifauny Shunatona Hines, who grew up on a reservation in Oklahoma and has lived in New York City for more than 10 years, says she will always feel connected to her heritage. "To me New York City is . . . Indian country for all those whose roots are elsewhere," she explains. "The ties are not cut, we have simply enlarged the endless Indian circle."

CONNECTING WITH THE HERITAGE

Over the past few decades, there has been a great increase in pow-wows, festivals, and ceremonies throughout the United States and Canada. These events offer an opportunity for American Indians to immerse themselves in the culture of their tribe, and sometimes other tribes as well. For example, North American Indian Days, a celebration held on the Blackfeet Reservation in Montana, brings together Indians from throughout North America. Regardless of the size of the event, it's clear that gatherings such as these play an important role in keeping Indian identity alive. As a dancer at a 2007 Seneca pow-wow said, "These three days refresh me and make me feel part again of our wonderful heritage."

Indians can choose to live traditional lifestyles or move to cities.

Members of the Tsimshian tribe raise a new totem pole at a senior center in Metlakatla, Alaska, emphasizing their connection with the past.

NEW INFORMATION NETWORKS

American Indians have also made good use of the Internet to forge connections with their past and their people. Individuals who are curious about their Indian ancestry can find out more on one of several websites devoted to the subject. Since the days of the *Cherokee Phoenix* (see p.126), Indian newspapers have continued to flourish, and many, such as the nationally circulated *Indian Country Today*, now have their own websites as well. People can even find life partners on online dating sites, many of which invite interested parties to "Meet Native American Singles."

MAKING DECISIONS

As they approach adulthood, all young people must choose the direction their lives will take. Often, young Indians face an especially difficult choice: Will they live in a city or suburb, working at a mainstream job, or will they follow a traditional lifestyle on a reservation? At a 2004 festival in Taos, New

Students on the Spokane Reservation in Washington work on their computer skills in the Wellpinit School's technology training center. All of the school's classrooms are connected to the Internet.

Mexico, a young Navajo named Steve Randall explained how he made his choice. Steve had done well in school, and he had been an outstanding athlete in football and track, so many expected him to leave the reservation behind.

"When I was growing up," he explained, "we didn't have running water, so I hauled water every day. I chopped firewood every day, too. It was kind of a challenge and it was fun. Now my little brother doesn't have to do those chores. He feels useless around the house, so he watches television and plays video games. It feels like we're losing so much.

"That's why I want to stay here. Our land is so beautiful, and we have prayers, dances, and music that celebrate that beauty. As long as I can make a living with crops and some sheep, why would I want to leave?"

A young Navajo shop owner disagreed. "We have to be part of the mainstream," he said. "We need industries and jobs and money. I grew up on the dirt floor of a hogan. We were so poor that a Boy Scout trip was a special treat because it meant three meals a day. I don't need to wear a headband or turquoise to prove I'm a good Navajo. And, as soon as I have enough money, I plan to move to New York and open a store selling Navajo products. The best of both worlds!"

ENTERING THE BUSINESS WORLD

In 2006, Florida's Seminole tribe purchased the Hard Rock Cafe chain of restaurants for $965 million. The move made headlines around the world. Even though Indian tribes had been investing in businesses for decades, it came as a shock to many people to think of a highly visible franchise like Hard Rock being owned by American Indians. For Tribe Vice Charman Max Osceola, this shock value was a welcome part of the deal, forcing the world to reevaluate its idea of what Indians were capable of. "Our ancestors sold Manhattan for trinkets," he told the press. "Today, with the acquisition of the Hard Rock Cafe, we're going to buy Manhattan back one hamburger at a time."

Since the acquisition, the money from Hard Rock is directed back to tribe's five reservations in Florida. Still, despite the tribe's success, many elders worry that the young Seminole are restless and eager to move to cities. To help keep

This banner was displayed at the Ahfachkee School on the Big Cypress Seminole reservation.

students connected to their history, the school on the Big Cypress reservation requires them to take daily culture classes, held in traditional thatch-roof chickees. "It's real important that we do help our children step into that modern world," says principal Terry Porter, "but at the same time try to help them understand [that you should] never forget where you came from, never forget what your people went through to get you where you're at today."

Two Navajo children snuggle up close at the Canyon de Chelly in Arizona. Like many of their fellow American Indians, these young people are growing up with more advantages than their parents had.

GLOSSARY

ADOBE
A building material made of sun-dried clay and straw

ALLOTMENT
A government program to divide Indian reservations up into plots of land owned by individuals

ASSIMILATION
A process in which individuals or communities from one culture adopt the language and customs of a dominant culture, which is usually associated with the state

ATLATL
A tool that throws a spear with greater power than can be achieved by hand

BLESSINGWAY
A Navajo ceremony intended to ensure good luck

BREECH-LOADING
Refers to a gun that is loaded from the back of the barrel, allowing for a shorter loading time

CALUMET
A long-stemmed pipe used in meetings with other tribes or important visitors

CESSION
A piece of land, or other propety, that is taken by the government for a specific purpose

CHANTWAY
A Navajo ceremony intended to restore health; usually involves making a sandpainting

CHERT
A type of flintlike rock used to make spear points

CHICKEE
A house built on stilts with open sides and a thatched roof; used by the Seminole and other Southeast tribes

CHIEF
The leader of a tribe. A tribe might have one or many chiefs, depending on the structure of its society.

CLAN
A group smaller than a tribe, made up of related families

CONQUISTADOR
A Spanish military leader during the conquest of the Americas, in the 16th and 17th centuries

COUNTING COUP
The practice of touching an enemy during battle, often with a coup stick, and then getting away unharmed; could also refer to other demonstrations of bravery

CRADLEBOARD
A rigid baby carrier that could be held on the back, attached to a horse, or propped up against a surface

DOG SOCIETY
A type of military society common among Plains tribes

DUGOUT CANOE
A canoe made by hollowing out a large log

FLAIL
A tool used to separate seeds from a plant

GREEN CORN CEREMONY
An important ceremony among Southeast tribes, held to give thanks for the ripened corn; also known as the busk

HEADDRESS
An elaborate covering for the head

HOGAN
A Navajo dwelling, usually made of logs with a domed mud roof and a door facing east

HOMESTEAD
A piece of land acquired from the government by virtue of settling and living there

IGLOO
A temporary dome-shaped Inuit hunting lodge, made of blocks of snow or ice

JERKY
A long-lasting trail food consisting of strips of meat dried in the sun or over a slow fire

KACHINA
A type of spirit believed to visit Pueblo villages

KAYAK
A one- or two-person Inuit canoe consisting of a frame covered with skins,

KIVA
An underground chamber where the Pueblo people held religious ceremonies

LACROSSE
A game in which two teams use sticks with netted ends to move a small ball across a field toward the other team's goal

LONGHOUSE
A long, communal dwelling used by the Iroquois and other Northeast tribes

MESA
A broad, flat-topped hill, common in the Southwest

MISSION
A religious center where members of the clergy try to convert native people to their religion

NORTHWEST PASSAGE
A theoretical water route connecting the Atlantic and Pacific Oceans, leading through or around North America

PALISADE
A fence made from a row of large pointed stakes

PARKA
A hooded jacket for use in extreme cold; also called an anorak

PEMMICAN
A long-lasting food made of dried meat, pounded and mixed with berries and animal fat

PERMAFROST
A layer of soil below the surface of extremely cold regions that remains frozen year round

PETROGLYPH
A carving or inscription made on the surface of a rock

POTLATCH
A ceremony among Northwest tribes in which a man demonstrated his status by giving away or destroying much of his property

POW-WOW
A modern American Indian gathering that features competitive dancing and other events

PUEBLO
A village of clustered houses or apartments made of adobe or stone, inhabited by the Pueblo people

RAWHIDE
Animal skin that has not been softened by tanning

RESERVATION
An area set aside by the U.S. government for the use of an Indian tribe; called a *reserve* in Canada

ROACH
A simple headdress made of dyed animal hair

SACHEM
A Northeast Indian chief

SANDPAINTING
A painting made of colored sand, traditionally created as part of a Navajo chantway ceremony and designed to last only one day

SHAMAN
A spiritual healer or leader whose power comes from contact with the spirit world

SMALLPOX
A disfiguring disease responsible for the deaths of thousands of Indians after contact with Europeans

SWEAT LODGE
A structure filled with steam, created by pouring water on hot stones; often used for ceremonial purposes

TEOSINTE
A wild grass thought to be the ancestor of modern corn

THREE SISTERS
The three main crops of many North American tribes: corn, beans, and squash; often grown together

TIPIS
Cone-shaped tents made of poles and animal hides, used as dwellings by Great Plains tribes

TOTEM
A symbol representing a family or clan

TOTEM POLE
A carved wooden pole created by tribes of the Pacific Northwest. The carvings can symbolize the history of a family, or other mythical or historical events.

TUNDRA
An Artic plain that remains frozen except for a few weeks in summer

TRAVOIS
A simple hauling device used by Plains tribes, consisting of a platform and two poles; drawn by dogs and later by horses

TREATY
A formal, written agreement between two or more nations

TRIBE
A group of people who share a common language, as well as customs and religious beliefs

ULU
An all-purpose Inuit knife with a semi-circular shape

WEIR
A fish trap consisting of a net stretched across a stream or river

WICKIUP
A dwelling used by Southwest tribes, consisting of a frame covered with grass, reeds, or brush

WIGWAM
A dwelling used by tribes in the Northeast; similar to a wickiup

WILD RICE
A North American grass with an edible grain; a relative of "true" rice, which is native to Asia and Africa

Books

Ceremony. Silko, Leslie Marmon. New York: Penguin, 1986.
This classic book tells the tale of an Indian man's struggle to readjust after fighting in World War II.

The Complete Idiot's Guide to Native American History. Fleming, Walter C. New York: Alpha Books, 2003.
You don't have to be an idiot to appreciate this informative guide to Indian history.

Do All Indians Live in Tipis? Mankiller, Wilma (Introduction). New York: HarperCollins, 2007.
Produced by the National Museum of the American Indian, this book dispels many misconceptions about Indians.

Eyewitness North American Indian. Murdoch, David. New York: DK Publishing, 2005.
Filled with amazing images of artifacts, this book provides an up-close look at Indian cultures.

The First Americans. Hakim, Joy. New York: Oxford University Press, 1993.
This book presents an engaging history of America's first people.

First Americans (series). King, David C. and others. Tarrytown, NY: Marshall Cavendish Benchmark Books, 2003–2009.
Each book in this series focuses on an individual tribe or nation.

More Than Moccasins: A Kid's Activity Guide to Traditional North American Indian Life. Carlson, Laurie. Chicago: Chicago Review Press, 1994.
This book is filled with hands-on activities such as making pottery or speaking in Navajo codes.

Native Nations of North America (series). Kalman, Bobbie and others. New York: Crabtree Publishing, 2001–2005.
This series looks at the people of the various Indian cultural regions.

North American Indians Today (series). Libal, Autumn. Broomall, PA: Mason Crest Publishers, 2003.
Each book in this series explores how a tribe lives in the modern world.

The Sign of the Beaver. Speare, Elizabeth George. Boston: Houghton Mifflin, 1983.
This award-winning novel tells the story of the friendship between a white boy and his Indian friend.

Places to visit

EAST

American Museum of Natural History
Central Park West and 79th Street
New York, NY 10024
www.amnh.org
The AMNH has excellent collections of Indian artifacts from many different regions.

Historical Museum of Southern Florida
101 West Flagler Street
Miami, FL 33130
www.hmsf.org
This museum features some 30,000 artifacts, mostly Seminole.

Horseshoe Bend National Military Park
11288 Horseshoe Bend Road
Daviston, AL 36256
www.nps.gov/hobe/
This park is located on the site of the overwhelming defeat of the Creek Nation in March 1814.

Iroquois Indian Museum
324 Caverns Road
Howes Cave, NY 12092
www.iroquoismuseum.org
This 45-acre nature park features many artifacts of Iroquois culture.

Mashantucket Pequot Museum and Research Center
110 Pequot Trail
Mashantucket, CT 06338
www.pequotmuseum.org
Made possible by revenue from the Foxwoods Casino, this museum features many interactive exhibits.

National Museum of the American Indian (Washington)
Fourth Street and Independence Avenue, S.W.
Washington, DC 20560
www.nmai.si.edu
With more than 800,000 objects in its collection, this is the first national museum dedicated exclusively to American Indians.

Peabody Museum of Archaeology and Ethnology
Harvard University
11 Divinity Avenue
Cambridge, MA 02138
www.peabody.harvard.edu
The Peabody features a large collection of archeological materials and a special exhibit on the history of Indian-White relations

Penn Museum
3260 South Street
Philadelphia, PA 19104
www.museum.upenn.edu
Operated by the University of Pennsylvania, this museum features artifacts from many Indian societies, including the Native people of Alaska.

The Schiele Museum of Natural History
1500 East Garrison Boulevard
Gastonia, NC 28054
www.schielemuseum.org
A variety of artifacts from 12 major culture areas in the United States and Canada make this an excellent destination.

MIDWEST

Cahokia Mounds State Historic Site
30 Ramey Street
Collinsville, IL 62234
www.cahokiamounds.com
See the incredible Monk's Mound, along with reconstructions of prehistoric Cahokia.

The Field Museum
1400 South Lake Shore Drive
Chicago, IL 60605
www.fieldmuseum.org
The museum's Ancient Americas exhibit takes you on a journey through 13,000 years of human achievement.

Glenbow Museum
130 Ninth Avenue Southeast
Calgary, Alberta T2G 0P3
Canada
www.glenbow.org
Here, visitors can learn about the cultures
of Canada's many Native tribes.

Little Bighorn Battlefield
Crow Agency, MT 59022
The site of the 1876 Battle of Little Bighorn
includes a visitor center with photographs,
maps, and exhibits.

Museum of the Fur Trade
6321 Highway 20
Chadron, NE 69337
www.furtrade.org
One of the continent's best collections of
fur trade artifacts can be found here.

Museum of the Plains Indian
Junction of U.S. Highways 2 and 89 West
Browning, MT
www.doi.gov/iacb/museums/museum_
plains.html
This collection includes many works by
contemporary artists and craftspeople.

Pawnee Indian Village Museum
480 Pawnee Trail
Republic, KS 66964
www.kshs.org/places/pawneeindian/
The main attraction is one the best-
preserved examples of an earth lodge.

WEST AND SOUTHWEST
Cabot's Pueblo Museum
67-616 East Desert View Avenue
Desert Hot Springs, CA 92240
www.cabotsmuseum.org
This Hopi-inspired pueblo contains artifacts
from many Indian cultures.

Denver Art Museum
100 West 14th Avenue Parkway
Denver, CO 80204
www.denverartmuseum.org
The DAM features the art and pottery of
the Hopi, Navajo, Blackfoot, and others.

Heard Museum
2301 North Central Avenue
Phoenix, AZ 85004
www.heard.org
From cultural objects to modern paintings,
the Heard Museum focuses exclusively on
American Indian art.

Mesa Verde National Park
Mesa Verde, CO 81330
www.nps.gov/meve/
Visit fantastic Anasazi cliff dwellings,
including the breathtaking Cliff Palace.

Museum of Indian Arts and Culture
710 Camino Lejo
Santa Fe, NM 87505
www.indianartsandculture.org
Located on Santa Fe's Museum Hill, this
museum tells the story of the Southwest's
Native people from prehistoric times
to today.

The Navajo Nation Museum
Highway 64 and Loop Road
Window Rock, AZ 86515
ggsc.wnmu.edu/mcf/museums/nnm.html
Operated by the Navajo nation, this
museum features nearly 5,000 objects
reflecting the history and culture of the
Navajo people.

Taos Pueblo
Taos, NM 87571
www.taospueblo.com
Visit a living, breathing Pueblo, where
Southwest Indians have lived for more
than 1,000 years.

NORTHWEST
Alaska State Museum
395 Whittier Street
Juneau, AK 99801
www.museums.state.ak.us
The first floor of this museum focuses on
artifacts from the Inuit, Aleut, and
Northwest cultures.

The Burke Museum of Natural History
and Culture
17th Avenue Northeast and Northeast
45th Street
Seattle, WA 98195
www.washington.edu/burkemuseum/
The University of Washington's natural
history museum features many exhibits on
the people of the Pacific Northwest.

Haida Heritage Centre
2 Second Beach Road
Skidegate, Haida Gwaii,
British Columbia V0T 1S1
Canada
Located on the Queen Charlotte Islands,
this museum features a wide array of Haida
artwork, including a gallery of totem poles.

Makah Museum
1880 Bayview Ave.
Neah Bay WA, 98357
www.makah.com
The tribal museum of the Makah people
features a full-size longhouse and artifacts
from an ancient Makah village.

Museum of Anthropology at the
University of British Columbia
6393 Northwest Marine Drive
Vancouver, British Columbia V6T 1Z2
Canada
www.moa.ubc.ca
This museum features exhibits from around
the world, but focuses on the First Nations
of the Northwest.

Seattle Art Museum
1300 First Avenue
Seattle, WA 98101
www.seattleartmuseum.org
This world-class museum features many
amazing artifacts from Northwest cultures.

Websites
Indianz.Com
www.indianz.com
This site provides news and opinions from
a Native American perspective. It provides
original content as well as links to other
news sites.

Indian Country Today
www.indiancountry.com
The online version of the leading national
American Indian newspaper has articles on
all aspects of Native culture.

Native Net
www.native-net.org
This website provides a wealth of
information on the history and culture of
many Native American tribes.

Native American Home Pages
www.nativeculturelinks.com
Lisa Mitten's web directory provides an
exhaustive list of Indian-related links.

CREDITS

IMAGE CREDITS

All the photographs in this book are used with permission and through the courtesy of:
(t=top, b=bottom, c=center, l=left, r=right)

DK IMAGES: 6–7b, 8–9, 16t, 19b, 23b, 34–35b, 42b, 46 (buffalo), 47 (fuel: chips), 50t (medicine wheel), 50b, 52r, 55 (fish, totem pole), 65b, 66–67, 70–71b, 71r, 73tc, 74 Dave King/Warwick Castle, 92 (turkey, strawberries, mint, cacao, corn, venison, peppers, pecans, popcorn, lima beans, green beans, wild rice, pumpkin, maple syrup, cranberries, rice, blueberries), 92 (kidney beans) Stephen Oliver, 92 (sunflower seeds) Dave King, 93 (jewelry, goldenseal, kayak, dogsled), 98 (rifle musket, Winchester rifle, Indian rifle, colt revolver), 98 (cartridge) Dave King, 103 (turquoise bracelets, turquoise necklace), 129 (wolf, basket, dog, pie, fish, horse, bread, buffalo, rattlesnake), 129 (eagle, bear) Dave King, 138; **Lynton Gardiner/ Courtesy of the American Museum of Natural History:** 1, 7t, 9r, 10 (deer, flail, mask, skull, dolls, pendant), 11 (anorak, snowshoes, husk face, lacross stick), 18, 21t, 28, 35tl, 35tr, 35c, 36 (pot, bracelets), 37tr, 40–41, 41bl, 43tl, 43b, 44br, 46 (clothing: belt, moccasins, headdress, shirt, long moccasins), (childcare: cradle board), 47 (containers: pipe bag, parfleche, saddlebag), (ceremonial objects: painted skull, ball, rattle drum, ghost dance wand, ceremonial case), (horseriding: saddle), (shelter: teepee), (warfare: shield), (tools: hammer), 48 (deer figure), 52l, 53tl, 55 (ceremonial hat), 56c, 57 (totem, grave house), 61 (boat, jacket, mask, pipe), 62–63b, 63tl, 65t, 69 (fan, house), 71bl, 73 (snowshoe, goggles, anorak), 86, 90tr, 93 (mask, moccasins, lacrosse stick), 95c, 96bl, 97br, 99 (bow & arrow, long-handled club, tomahawk), 100t, 102t, 107cr, 108t, 110–111, 111t, 111tr, 113tr, 115cr, 139 (helmet, roach, shaman's headdress, feather crown, horn bonnet), 144, 146r

GETTY IMAGES: 2–3, 14 Fred Hirschmann, 26t Aztec; 26b DEA/G. DAGLIORTI; 49b, 63tr, 64bl, 80–81, 103cl, 118c, 142–143, 149b, 150, 151, 155b, 160b, 161b, 165, 172tr, 175tr, 177t Getty Images; 82–83 National Geographic; 155t, 156, 168b Time & Life Pictures; 158 Suzanne Murphy; 169b National Geographic; 172tl Diamond Images

BRIDGEMAN ART LIBRARY: 4–5, 91r, 94–95b 107br, 125r Private Collection; 65cr Peabody Essex Museum; 77tl Service Historique de la Marine/Lauros/Giraudon; 93 (blanket), 101b Fred Jones Jr. Museum of of Art, University of Oklahoma; 114tl Bibliotheque des Arts Decoratif, Paris; 118–119t Ashmolean Museum; 130–131 Woolaroc Museum; 134 Kennedy Gallery; 136b University of Michigan Museum of Art

ALAMY IMAGES: 6t, 16b David Lyons; 17 Peter Arnold; 19t, 60–61b, 62t, 78l, 79tr, 84t, 85b, 91l 89tr, 95t, 100–101b, 115tr, 120tr, 121t, 122b, 124t, 126, 133t, 181tr Northwind Picture Archive; 20r Ambient Images; 21b, 62c, 71tl The Print Collector; 22 World Pictures; 23t, 63c, 87–88b 120 tl, 127t, 140 Mary Evans Picture Library; 24–25 Sue Clark; 27br Classic Image; 31t Tom Till; 31c, 51c, 104–105 Robert Harding Picture Library; 36tr Nicholas Pitt; 36–37 Mervyn Rees; 39tl CuboImages srl; 39 (sandpainting), 178–179 Chuck Place; 40b Don B. Stevenson; 41cr Saulius T. Kondrotas; 42–43, 43tr, 49t INTERFOTO Pressbildagentor; 44–45, 68b, 77 (ceremonial dancing, Roanoke chief), 79tl, 121b, 125l Visual Arts Library, London; 47 (food: jerky foodfolio, fresh meat) James Nesterwitz; 48b Julius Fekete; 49tr, 58–59 Tom Mackie; 51tl Robert E. Barber; 51tr David Frazier; 53tc Graphic Science; 54 Todd Bannor, 55b (fish Keith Douglas); 56b John T. Marriott; 64–65, 96tl, 115tl INTERFOTO; 72b David Norton Photography; 85b Thomas Hallstein; 90b blickwinkel; 92 (jerky) foodfolio; 93 (Echinacea) TH Foto; 93 (cascara) Geoffrey Kidd; 93 (dreamcatcher) Emilio Ereza; 93 (toboggan) Alaska Stock; 106b framzfoto.com; 106t ML Pearson; 107 Richard Cummins; 109 (beaver) Greg Vaughn; 124b Thomas K. Fletcher; 169, 175tl Andre Jenny; 176l Hemis; 180 Mira

Michigan Technological University/Archchaeology Laboratory: 20l Patrick E. Martin; 20r Susan R. Martin

CORBIS: 27c The Gallery Collection; 30 Werner Forman; 45br Time & Life Pictures; 49tl Corbis; 53b, 174–175b Marilyn Angel Wynn/Native Stock Pictures; 56t, 110b, 111b Canadian Museum of Civilization; 76 Poodles Rock; 78r, 119br, 161t, 162–163b, 163c, 164t, 166–167 Bettman; 81tl Steven Clevenger; 81tr Kevin Fleming; 91br Michael Maslin Historic Photographs; 93 Peter Harholdt; 108–109 Museum of History and Industry; 109 (sweathouse) Underwood & Underwood; 113br Christie's Images; 118b Richard T. Nowitz; 157t Museum of History & Industry; 168t Anders Ryman; 170 Buddy Mays; 171t Bob Krist; 176r; 181tl Ed Kashi; 181b B.S.I.

LIBRARY OF CONGRESS: 27t, 39cr, 41b, 44bl 51b, 53tr, 55 (Makah whalers), 57b, 68r, 73b, 81b, 96–97, 101tr, 102l, 103b, 107t, 112–113, 113cl, 114–115b, 119tr, 122t, 123tl, 123br, 127bl, 127br, 131, 133br, 134t, 135r, 136t, 137b, 141b, 146l, 147t, 147b, 148, 149t, 153t, 154t, 154b, 154t, 160t, 163t

CAHOKIA MOUNDS STATE HISTORIC SITE: 31b, 32–33

ART RESOURCE: 37 (pitcher), 112t Werner Forman

AMERICAN MUSEUM OF NATURAL HISTORY: 38tr, 57 (Haida shamans)

EITELJORG MUSEUM: 38c

DENVER PUBLIC LIBRARY: 38–39, 94t, 152–153

BUFFALO BILL HISTORICAL CENTER: 46 (clothing: robe, bonnet, bonnet), (childcare: doll); 47 (containers: storage bag, bowl, pouch), (ceremonial objects: cupping horn, drum), (horseriding: rope), (warfare: war club), (tools: berry masher, hide scraper, utensils, flesher, spoon, paintbrushes), 99 (coup stick (Chandler-Pohrt Coll., gift of Mr. & Mrs. Richard A. Pohrt), war club (Dr. Robert L. Anderson Collection, NA. 108. 39), decorated club, lance (NA. 205. 38); 116, 141 (Gift: Robert G. Charles, NA. 702. 4), 139 (buffalo bonnet), 141t

MINNESOTA HISTORICAL SOCIETY: 65cl

THE GRANGER COLLECTION: 69t, 78–79b, 120

NATIVE STOCK PICTURES: 70t Marilyn Angel Wynn

WASHINGTON HISTORICAL SOCIETY: 85t

HUDSON BAY COMPANY ARCHIVES: 90tl

ALASKA STATE LIBRARY: 109 (cannon)

ARCHITECT OF THE CAPITOL: 123bl

UTAH HISTORICAL SOCIETY: 132–133

PALACE OF THE GOVERNORS: 135t PHOTO ARCHIVES (NMHM/DCA), 044516

JOHN F. KENNEDY LIBRARY AND ARCHIVES: 157b

ASSOCIATED PRESS: 164b, 171b, 172–73t, 173tr. 177b

MEDAL OF HONOR SOCIETY: 173b

TIMELINE: 12: left to right: Row 1: **Alamy**/Peter Arnold, Row2: **Alamy**/Northwind, **Alamy**/Mervyn Rees, **Alamy**/Northwind; Row 3: **Library of Congress, Bridgeman**/Fred Jones Jr. Museum of Art; Row 4: **Bridgeman**/Woolaroc Museum. 13 left to right: Row 1: **Alamy**/Peter Arnold, **Alamy**/Tom Till; Row 2: **DK Images**/ Lynton Gardiner/Courtesy of the American Museum of Natural History, **Corbis**/ Steven Clevenger, **Alamy**/World Pictures; Row 3: **Alamy**/North Wind Picture Archives, **Alamy**/North Wind Picture Archives, **Alamy**/North Wind Picture Archives; Row 4: **Getty Images, Alamy**/North Wind Picture Archives, **Alamy**/Jim West; Row 5: **Corbis**/Bettman

Front Cover Photo by **Corbis**

Front Cover Flap by **DK Images**

Cover Flap Borders: **DK Images**/Lynton Gardiner/Courtesy of the American Museum of Natural History

Back Cover Photos: Totem Pole: **Getty Images**/Altrendo Travel; Shield: **DK Images**/Lynton Gardiner/Courtesy of the American Museum of Natural History; Moccasins: **DK Images**/Lynton Gardiner/Courtesy of the American Museum of Natural History

Back Cover Flap by **Getty Images**

Spine: **Getty Images**/David C. Tomlinson

Page borders: **DK Images**/David Mager: Front/backmatter, Chapter 1, Chapter 2, Chapter 3, Chapter 4; **DK Images**/Gunter Marx/Courtesy of Stanley Park, Totem Park, Vancouver, British Columbia: Chapter 5; **DK Images**/Lynton Gardiner/Courtesy of the American Museum of Natural History: Chapter 6, Chapter 7

Leather background: **DK Images**/David Mager

WORKS CITED

p.45 (Preparing Bison Hides) Catlin, George. *Life among the Indians*, New York: Gall & Inglis, 1875; reprinted in Jon E. Lewis, *The Mammoth Book of Native Americans*. New York: Carroll & Graf, 2004, pp.31–32.

p.80 ("a little crowded village . . .") Miller, James and John Thompson. *National Geographic Almanac of American History*. Washington, D.C.: National Geographic, 2005, p.59.

p.80 ("something that we prized much more . . ." "your main purpose . . .") De Castaneda, Pedro. "Narrative of Pedro de Castaneda." *Fourteenth Annual Report of the Bureau of American Ethnology*, Washington, D.C.: U.S. Government Printing Office, 1896; reprinted in Lewis, p.53.

p.95 (Buffalo Hunting) Standing Bear, Luther. *My People, The Sioux*. Boston: Houghton Mifflin, 1928; reprinted in Krupat, Arnold. *Native American Autobiography: An Anthology*. Madison, WI: University of Wisconsin Press, 1994, pp.202–203.

p.97 (Roomier lodgings) Catlin, *Life Among the Indians*; reprinted in Lewis, pp.30–31.

p.109 ("The survivors were most terribly pitted . . .") Mann, Charles C. "1492: America Before Columbus Was More Sophisticated and More Populous Than We Have Ever Thought." *The Atlantic Monthly*, March 2002; reprinted in Johansen, Bruce E. *The Native Peoples of North America: A History*. New Brunswick, NJ: Rutgers University Press, 2005, p.225.

p.118 ("Why will you destroy us . . .") Jackson, Helen Hunt. *A Century of Dishonor: A Sketch of the United States Government's Dealings with Some of the Indian Tribes*. New York: Harper & Brothers, 1881; quoted in Johansen, p.62.

p.121 ("My heart is broken") Quoted in Johansen, p.94.

p.121 ("He gave me a pancake . . .") Rowlandson, Mary. *A Narrative of the Captivity, Sufferings, and Removes of Mrs. Mary Rowlandson*. Boston: 1777; reprinted in Utley, Robert M. and Wilcomb E. Washburn. *The American Heritage History of the Indian Wars*. New York: Bonanza Books, 1977, p.59.

p.130–131 ("We were drove off like wolves . . ." "Families at dinner were startled . . .") Quoted in Lewis, pp.141–142.

p.131 ("We learned from the inhabitants . . .") Ehle, John. *Trail of Tears: The Rise & Fall of the Cherokee Nation*. New York: Doubleday, 1988, p.212.

p.133 ("All over the plains, lying in disgusting masses . . .") Webb, William. *Buffalo Land*. Cincinnati & Chicago: E. Hannaford & Co., 1872; reprinted in King, David C. *American Heritage/American Voices: Westward Expansion*. Hoboken, NJ: John Wiley & Sons, 2003, pp.202–203.

p.137 ("Destroy everything they own . . .") Quoted in Johansen, p.264.

p.137 ("I have come to kill Indians . . .") Quoted in Lewis, p.177.

p.137 ("Nothing lives long . . .") Chief White Antelope, quoted in Lewis, p.182.

p.141 ("It is cold and we have no blankets . . .") King, *Westward Expansion*, pp.123–124.

p.147 ("What we saw was terrible . . .") Collier, John. *Indians of the Americas*. New York: New American Library, 1947, pp.104–105.

p.147 ("Once more the men of the Seventh Cavalry . . .") Quoted in Johansen, p.287.

p.148 ("Kill the Indian and save the man . . .") Quoted in Johansen, p.308.

p.149 ("teach young . . .") Pratt, Richard Henry. *Battlefield and Classroom*. Edited by Robert Utley. Lincoln, Nebraska: University of Nebraska Press, 1987, p.235.

p.149 (The Struggle to Adjust) Standing Bear, Luther. *Land of the Spotted Eagle*. Boston: Houghton Mifflin, 1933, pp.318–321.

p.153 ("Into this vat . . .") Quoted in Lewis, p.329.

p.153 (Cutting It Short) "Apaches and Their Hair." *New York Times*, June 27, 1897.

p.155 ("Placed in bondage . . .") Quoted in Johansen, p.332.

p.168 ("When they're not sleeping . . .") Gamble, Susan. "Shocked at Conditions in Reserve." *Brantford Expositor*; quoted in Johansen, p.390.

p.171 ("If you desecrate . . .") Thomas, David Hurst. *Skull Wars: Kennewick Man, Archaeology, and the Battle for Native American Identity*. New York: Basic Books, 2000, p.210.

p.173 ("a tendency to bring Native Americans into contempt . . .") Chicago-Kent College of Law, "Harjo v. Pro-Football, Inc." http://www.kentlaw.edu/student.orgs/jip/trade/skins.htm

p.173 ("stand tall, admit it was wrong . . .") Quoted in Johansen, p.421.

p.180 ("To me New York City is . . .") Quoted in King, David C. *The United States and Its People*. New York: Prentice Hall, 1995, p.812.

p.180 ("These three days refresh . . .") *Buffalo News*, July 23, 2007.

p.181 ("When I was growing up . . ." "We have to be part of the mainstream . . .") Quoted in King, David C. *First Americans: The Navajo*. Tarrytown, NY: Marshall Cavendish, 2008, pp.38–39.

p.181 ("Today, with the acquisition . . .") "Seminoles will purchase Hard Rock Cafe business." *Boston Globe*, December 8, 2006.

p.181 (" It's real important . . .") Saiz, Adrian. "Seminole's business brings change to Reservation." Associated Press/News from Indian Country, April 2007.

ACKNOWLEDGMENTS

The author would like to thank John Searcy and Beth Sutinis for guiding this project from the start, Anne Burns for outstanding picture research, and the design and production staffs at DK. And special thanks to my lovely wife Sharon for all her encouragement, support, and hard work.

The publisher would like to thank Dr. Peter M. Whiteley for his thorough and expeditious consulting work on this project. Thanks also to Anne Burns for her picture research, David Mager for his photography, and Ed Merritt for his outstanding work on the maps.

ABOUT THE AUTHOR

David C. King has a BA and MA in history and political science from the State University of New York at Buffalo. He has taught high-school history and English, and has served as a consultant to the Corporation for Public Broadcasting, the New York State Department of Education, the National Council for the Social Studies, the Foreign Policy Association, and the Lincoln Center Institute for the Arts in Education. He has written more than 70 books for children and adults, including DK's *Children's Encyclopedia of American History*, and has won a number of awards.

ABOUT THE CONSULTANT

Peter M. Whiteley is the Curator of North American Ethnology at the American Museum of Natural History in New York. He has a PhD in anthropology from the University of New Mexico, and currently serves as an Adjunct Professor of Anthropology at Columbia University, and an editorial board member of *American Anthropologist*, the journal of the American Anthropological Association. In his research, Dr. Whiteley studies cultures, social structures, social histories, and environmental relations in Native North America from the 17th century to the present. His recent work has focused on the Pueblo people.